"Thomas Marshall has writter

designed for students and laymen alike. As a pastor, I can recommend this work written from a view that takes the Bible as the inerrant, infallible Word of God, necessary for biblical knowledge and practical for life."

> Jerry Falwell
> Pastor
> Thomas Road Baptist Church
> Founder and Chancellor
> Liberty University, Lynchburg, Virginia

"Thomas Marshall has written an extremely practical New Testament survey for use by students. This will prepare a student for a lifelong of study in the Word of God. This book is written from a conservative view that takes the Bible as the literal Word of God. The author emphases the historic Christian church that believes the Great Commission should be obeyed and that Christians should live holy lives. This is an outstanding base from which to teach students to obey the Word of God and the Great Commission."

> Elmer L. Towns
> Vice President, Liberty University
> Dean, School of Religion

"Dr. Marshall is wonderful teacher of the Bible, and his *A Student's New Testament Survey* puts onto paper what he loves to teach about and help students learn. His survey helps students see God's purpose as a whole for His people with clear explanation and the right amount of detail to grasp the big picture. I am pleased to recommend this tool to homeschooled students who desire to see how the New Testament is connected to all of God's plans and to have a better understanding of the main idea of each New Testament book."

> Sandra Sauerwein
> Director, Chieftain Institute
> Derwood Bible Church

"Dr. Marshall is a friend, colleague, and now author who has proven himself over time to be effective in communicating God's truth. As a former history and Bible teacher, I find this work to be accurate, trustworthy, and one that I would use. Regardless of your denomination or doctrinal positions, this work will be an asset to one's personal study or use in a classroom setting. I commend Dr. Marshall for this inspiring and informational work."

> John W. Storey, Ed.D.
> ACSI Regional Director

A STUDENT'S
New Testament Survey

A STUDENT'S

New Testament Survey

Dr. Thomas Marshall

TATE PUBLISHING & *Enterprises*

Published by Tate Publishing & Enterprises, LLC
127 E. Trade Center Terrace | Mustang, Oklahoma 73064 USA
1.888.361.9473 | www.tatepublishing.com

Tate Publishing is committed to excellence in the publishing industry. The company reflects the philosophy established by the founders, based on Psalms 68:11,
"The Lord gave the word and great was the company of those who published it."

Book design copyright © 2007 by Tate Publishing, LLC. All rights reserved.
Cover design by Jennifer Redden
Interior design by Brandon Wood
Published in the United States of America

ISBN: 978-1-6024735-2-2
07.06.15

—∾—

This book is dedicated to the memory of
Thomas J. Marshall, who taught me
a love for God and His Word
and whom I called *Dad*.

Acknowledgments

When preparing a work like this, it is impossible to acknowledge all who have played a part in the culmination of a dream. Over the years, I have constantly studied under many different instructors who have brought the Bible alive. If I sought to include everyone, I am sure to miss someone.

I do want to briefly acknowledge some who are instrumental in this work. First, I want to thank Mid-Atlantic Baptist Institute for the initial trust in me to teach God's Word. It was there that this work was conceived. Over the years, the opportunity to preach and teach at Trinity Baptist Church and Montrose Baptist Church has been invaluable. I want to recognize Montrose Christian School where I have taught Bible from the elementary to high school over the years. Their faith and trust in my instruction is very much appreciated.

I need to acknowledge my mom and honor the memory of my dad in this work. They started my love for God and His Word. Over the years they have put up with a lot from me, and always lovingly guided me back to where I needed to be. Thanks, Mom. Dad, as you peer down from heaven, I love and miss you.

I want to thank especially my wife, Linda, for her constant encouragement to strive forward when often I felt like giving up. My daughters have been a consistent source of enjoyment and I have always felt that I can "bounce" ideas off them before I make a bigger fool of myself than I already am.

I appreciate Emily Jefferis, who took the time to proofread this manuscript and make suggestions. I also appreciate the encouragement and patience of the Montrose Christian Lower School teachers while I worked on this book.

I also want to acknowledge the team of people from Tate Publishing who have taken this book from a dream to a reality. I wish to show appreciation to Stacy Baker in Acquisitions, Jesika Lay in Operations, Dave Dolphin in Publications, and many others who have put time and thought into the final outcome of this work. I want to particularly express thanks to my editor, Kylie Lyons, for the painstaking task of reviewing, correcting, offering encouragement, suggestions, and in general making this poor writer look good. Without the team, I would not have made it, I am therefore very grateful.

Table of Contents

The material presented in this student's survey has been gathered from many different sources for many different years. It will not always be possible to acknowledge the source of the information, but I want to thank all my teachers, mentors, fellow pastors, and others who have had a part in this project.

There are many good Surveys out on the market. This is not to take away from them, but I am attempting to present the material from a student's perspective. This is a traditional Baptistic view, one that sees the church beginning with Jesus, the local Church as the instrument through which God worked and works, that places emphasis upon evangelism and missions, recognizing Jesus as the central theme, and that holds to the fact that the Bible *is* God's Word.

I pray that as I travel through the world of the New Testament with you, we will both be blessed by what we learn.

What do you see when you come to study the Bible? Is it a dusty, old book full of difficult ideas, or is it alive and vibrant for today? Many times people have trouble understanding the Bible because they are looking at each individual verse instead of seeing the whole picture.

Consider this picture:

There is a parade passing down the main street of your hometown. You can hear the bands and the excitement is in the air. However, the parade is on the other side of a large, solid, wooden fence. You cannot see it at all. Then, you notice a knothole in the fence, and you peer through it. You see the majorettes pass by. Then the band, they are followed by the floats—one at a time—and finally the clowns pass by. If someone were to ask you what made up the parade, you would probably answer whatever you saw at that moment. However, your best friend is sitting on top of the fence, and he can see it all at once. What a difference in the perspective and understanding.

That is where this study comes in. There are three phases of Bible study. *Observation*—seeing what the text says, *Interpretation*—determining what it means, and *Application*—applying the text to our lives. A survey is an overall view of the Bible, or the *Observation* phase of study.

In our survey, we want to see each part in relation to all the other parts for the correct interpretation and emphasis. There is an old hermeneutical principal that states, "A text without a context is a pretext." We need to observe the total structure of the book, the content of the book, get a feel for the atmosphere of the book, see how it relates to the Bible as a whole, and then derive spiritual lessons from the book's overall thrust.

To do this, we want to move from out of the fog and into the sunlight. Start by scanning the entire book of the Bible. Get a pencil and paper, jot down your first impressions. Look for key words, phrases, ideas. Then, as you continue to read the Book, divide it into sections. Put a title on each section and record any observations that you have about that section.

We want to see how it all fits together. We need in this day not only to know what God said (the content), but how He said it (the structure).

As we begin our study, let us pause to consider the background to the writings we have today that we call our Bible. If we say that this is God's Word, how did we get it? Can we trust it? Is this all that God has to say?

These questions cannot be answered in depth in this book, but a starting point can be given, and I encourage the serious student of God's Word to look deeper into these areas.

A. Three Aspects

First, in the delivery of God's Word to us, there are three aspects. These are Revelation, Inspiration, and Illumination.

Revelation is God's communication of truth to man. You could call this "from God to man," it is man hearing what God wants written. The word *revelation* means an uncovering, the drawing away of the veil. This is what God did in revealing His Word to men. He used at least eight different means of communication to us. These eight means are:

1. through Angels - Luke 2:8–14
2. through a clear voice - Exodus 20:1–17
3. through a still, small voice - 1 Kings 19:11–12.
4. through Nature - Psalm 19:1–3
5. through the mouth of an ass - Numbers 22:28
6. through Dreams - Matthew 1:20
7. through Visions - Isaiah 6:1–8
8. through Christophonies - Exodus 3:2[1]

After God spoke to man, then man needed to write what God wanted written. This is getting it "from man onto paper." The term for this is *Inspiration*. There are various theories that deal with inspiration.

Some of these theories briefly are:

1. Natural Theory - states that writers were inspired the way Shakespeare was. 2 Peter 1:20 disputes this.
2. Mechanical Theory - God coldly dictated the Bible like an office manager would to a secretary. The different vocabularies dispute that idea.
3. Concept Theory - only the main concepts were inspired. Matthew 5:18 disputes this idea.
4. Partial Theory - only certain parts were inspired. 2 Timothy 3:16 teaches that *all* the Bible is inspired.
5. Spiritual Rule Only Theory - that the Bible is infallible in concerns of Faith, but not in other matters. John 3:12 should be read in conjunction with that idea.
6. Plenary-Verbal Theory - that all (plenary) the very words (verbal) of the Bible are inspired by God. Read 2 Timothy 3:16, 17 to see this. God used the personalities of the writers to pen exactly what He wanted.[2]

We must, at this point, also stress that Inspiration stopped when John finished writing Revelation 22:21.

This brings us to the final aspect, *Illumination*. The final part of God's plan is man receiving that which was written. It is "from paper to heart." It is necessary because the Bible teaches of the natural blindness of man,[3] Satanic blindness,[4] and carnal blindness.[5] The results of illumination are that sinners are saved[6] and the saints are strengthened.[7]

One last statement in dealing with illumination, the

Holy Spirit seeks the aid of believers to perform His task of illumination in the hearts of others. There are three things needed for salvation:

1. The Spirit of God
2. The Word of God
3. The Child of God to get the Word out

B. Transmission

The study of the transmission of the text of God's Word is a very detailed endeavor. By transmission, we mean the process by which the Biblical manuscripts have been copied down through the ages by hand or machine. At times scribal errors have crept into the copies, but God has preserved the text from doctrinal error all the way to this present time.

As Divine Author, God wrote an infallible book (inspiration); as Divine Protector, He has preserved the text from doctrinal error (transmission).[8]

C. Canon

Canonization is the identification of a writing as being part of the Scriptures. The word *canon* comes from a word that means "rule or guide."

There were essentially five tests that a book had to pass to be included in the canon of Scripture. According to Dr. H. L. Wilmington of Liberty University, the books we have today were submitted to the tests of:

1. Authorship
2. Local Church Acceptance
3. Recognition by the early Church Fathers
4. The content of the Book subject matter, and
5. Personal edification.

All books had to pass all five tests to be considered Canonical. Some of the books we have today were first doubted, but were eventually settled upon. The Old Testament Canon was finalized by 300 BC (some believe that Ezra was responsible for it). The New Testament was finalized during the Third Council of Carthage in 397 AD.

D. Translations

The area of Bible translations is a very heated topic among Christians. We do not have the original manuscripts (possibly because God knows how we tend to worship idols), and thus we have the debate over which one(s) of the translations is best.

The Latin Vulgate (384 AD) was the most important ancient translation; in fact, the first English translation was based upon this Latin version. There were many early English versions produced, and some cost their translators their lives. This was particularly true during the Reformation.

The King James Version (KJV) was commissioned to end the feuding over which translation to use. Fifty-four Anglican scholars over a period of seven years translated the work. They used Erasmus' Greek text (translated back from the Latin text in places), which was referred to as the "Textus Receptus" in an advertisement for Erasmus' translation. Many of the Anglican Church doctrines were included in the translation. It is called today the "Authorized Version" because King James—the leader of the Anglican Church—commissioned the translation. The KJV that we hold today has gone through four revisions since 1611. The New King James Version is revision five. Some of the reasons why there have been revisions are:

- The change of the English language since 1611
- New Manuscripts have been discovered
- Increased Knowledge of Hebrew and Greek.

The major differences between translations hinge on the manuscript fragments used, whether the translators insisted upon a literal or dynamic-equivalence translation, and/or any possible dogmatic views with which a group may be concerned. A literal translation basically attempts to translate the words directly into English; a dynamic-equivalent translation attempts to translate the thoughts based upon the wording; and a paraphrase attempts to translate the thoughts based upon the contextual setting. The chart on this page divides the more popular translations into their respective forms.

Literal	Dynamic Equivalent	Paraphrase
King James Version (KJV)	New International Version (NIV)	Phillips
New King James Version (NKJV)	Jerusalem Bible (JB)	Today's Living Bible (TLB)
Revised Standard Version (RSV)	Revised English Bible (REV)	
American Standard Version (ASV)	New American Bible (NAB)	
New American Standard Version (NASB)	Good News Bible (GNB)	
Holman Christian Standard Version (HCSB)		

The New Revised Standard Version (NRSV) and the New Living Translation (NLT) are a combination of the Dynamic Equivalent and the Paraphrase approach to translation.

I hope that the readers will take the time to study the issue relating to Biblical Versions and will settle for themselves the issue as God leads them.

A. Political

There were three political entities in this world at the time of Christ. They were the Roman, the Hellenistic, and the Jewish states. The first two were closely tied together, and the third kept its sovereignty from the others. Let us begin with the state of the Romans.

Roman Empire

The empire of Rome was founded in 753 BC as a small union of villages. Nevertheless, in a little over two hundred years, it had a strong republican form of government. Rome became the ruler of Italy by defeating the Etruscans in 265 BC. They conquered Carthage in 146 BC, which made them a chief maritime power. They proceeded to conquer Achaia in 146 BC. Following the death of Attalus III of Pergamum, they acquired the territory of Asia in 133 BC. In 63 BC, they annexed Syria and Judea; finally, in 57 BC, they conquered Gaul. In a period of five hundred years of uninterrupted war, the empire of Rome grew from an obscure village to a ruling empire. In fact, there were constant Civil Wars until 30 BC when Octavian became Emperor.

As we are mentioning Emperors, there are thirteen that we need to stop and consider.

The Emperors of Rome

Augustus - Emperor from 27 BC to 14 AD. He was the first to be called the Princeps, or first citizen of Rome.

He ruled wisely and established the compromise between republicanism and a dictatorship. In 27 BC, he became the commander in chief, and in 23 BC, he was given Tribunal power for life. He is noted for many outstanding events in his life. He was responsible for having the Senate purged of unworthy members, he started the professional Army, the Julian Laws (19 and 18 BC) were established to improve family life, he organized the police and fire departments, and he boasted that he found Rome brick and left it marble. The most important event in this study is that Augustus was the ruler at the time of Christ's birth.[9]

Tiberius - Emperor from 14 to 37 AD. He became emperor at fifty-six years of age, after spending most of his life in politics. He had been forced to marry Julia, the daughter of Augustus, and became very bitter about it. His reign was marked by his distant, haughty, and suspicious nature. This caused him to be generally disliked. He is the emperor that was on the throne during the ministry of Jesus.

Caligula - Emperor from 37 to 41 AD. Affectionately known by his soldiers as "Little Boots." Possibly this was a nickname given to him as a child because he loved to wear military boots. He was very popular because he reduced the taxes that Romans had to pay. Nevertheless, he was mentally weak and soon demanded to be worshipped as a god. He ordered his statue erected in the Temple at Jerusalem, which did not go over very well. His reckless expenditures depleted the treasury, and he was forced to resort to violent means to restore the viability of the treasury. His life was cut short when he was assassinated by the Imperial Guard.

Claudius - Emperor from 41 to 54 AD. An early illness

(possibly Infantile Paralysis) left Claudius looking idiotic. He was lame and had a stuttering problem. His redeeming virtue was that he was a brilliant scholar. He sought to restore the ancient Roman religion. The Roman historian Suetonius lists that he expelled some Jews from Rome for the reason that riots were taking place because "of one Chrestus." It was possibly during this time that Aquila and Priscilla were expelled from Rome.[10] He was the Emperor on the throne during Paul's ministry.

Nero - Emperor from 54 to 68 AD. A very interesting study can be made about this man. The first five years of his reign were quiet. Then, in 59 AD, to gain total control he had his mother murdered. From this point on, his reign was one of turmoil. He was an artist, and not one of executive material. His carelessness and extravagance emptied the treasury of Rome. In 64 AD, a great fire swept through Rome leaving it blackened and devastated. Nero is thought to be the one behind it, because he wanted to build a Golden House and needed to clear the way for it. A scapegoat was needed, so he accused the Christians and many were subsequently brought to trial. It was during this persecution that Peter and Paul perished. Nero finally had to flee and was put to death by his own order to avoid being captured. We look back at Nero in New Testament study and see him as the one who started the Roman persecution of Christians and was responsible for Paul's death.

Gaba, Otho, and Vitellius - three short-lived emperors. Gaba was emperor in 68 AD and was killed by his guards under the order of Otho. Otho ruled in 69 AD and was killed in battle. Vitellius also ruled in 69 AD but was unable to control his own soldiers. The troops of Vespasian sacked Rome, killed Vitellius and allowed Vespasian to come to power.

Vespasian - Emperor from 69 AD to 79 AD. After establishing his power, he proceeded to suppress the revolts in Batvia and Gaul, while his General Titus flattened Jerusalem. He established a solvent treasury by a very strict economy. With his strict economy, he was able to construct the Coliseum at Rome. He is important to students of New Testament study because he was on the throne at the time Jerusalem was overthrown and destroyed.

Titus - Emperor from 79 to 81 AD. He was the General who led the troops to destroy the capital city Jerusalem. Under him, the Temple of Jerusalem was burned and razed to the ground.[11] He was very popular with the people, mainly because he loved to provide public entertainment. One time, when Rome suffered a fire that destroyed the Capitol, Parthenon, and Agrippa's Baths, Titus sold his private possessions to meet the general need. However, as students of New Testament study, we must remember that he is the man who destroyed Jerusalem.

Domitian - Emperor who ruled from 81 to 96 AD. He was a brother to Titus. In the role of emperor, he was an autocrat. He tried to raise the public moral level by restraining prostitution in Rome. However, he soon demanded to be worshipped as a god. He was hailed as *Dominus et Deus*.[12] He was a good economist in the public realm. His nature was one that was hard and suspicious, making him pitiless in his revenge. He felt that he had numerous enemies so that even his own family felt unsafe and had him assassinated. He is probably the emperor that sat on the throne while John wrote the book of Revelation.

Nerva - Emperor from 96 to 98 AD. He was a man of

advanced years when he came to the throne. He was considered a "safe" candidate to rule the empire. His administration was kindly and free from internal tensions.

Trajan - Emperor from 98 to 117 AD. He was a Spaniard by birth and a soldier by profession. He was energetic and aggressive in his temperament.

These emperors sat on the throne of Rome during the time of the New Testament. From Augustus to Trajan, God used the pagan world and what it thought was its own schemes and plans to forward His great plan. The plan of the ages—that Jesus would provide salvation, and the Church that He established while here on earth would carry the good news to the ends of the known world of that day.

Provincial Government

The Roman Empire was made up of a miscellaneous realm of independent cities, states, and territories. All except Italy was under the Provincia from which we get our word *province*. The provincia was a "post of command," and it was a territory that a general had conquered.

There were two forms of government. The Proconsuls were the peaceful provinces and answered to the Roman state. The Procurator was for the turbulent provinces and was answerable to the Emperor himself. The offices of procurator were on an annual appointment basis. Pilate, before whom Jesus was tried, was a procurator.

The Hellenistic Kingdom

Roman culture owed its origin to the political organization of Rome and to the Hellenistic spirit of the day. The Roman conquests had absorbed the Greek colonies. This brought great treasures to Rome. In addition, the inclusion of the Greek slaves brought in many who were more intelligent than their Roman masters were. They were employed as teachers, doctors, accountants, and other mentally skilled jobs. The Greek universities were attended by the Roman aristocrats who, in turn, learned Greek.

The most important of the Hellenists was Alexander the Great. His father was Philip, King of Macedonia. In just twenty years, Philip had succeeded in making the Greek city-states servant to Macedonia. Then Philip died in 337 BC. His son Alexander possessed his father's aggressive military genius. He also had a good veneer of Greek culture from studying under Aristotle.

In 334 BC, he defeated the Persian forces at Granicus River. He then gained control of Asia Minor. He followed this by subduing Syria and Egypt, where he founded the city of Alexandria. He spent three years consolidating his empire.

The luxury and revel of Babylon weakened him. It is said that he cried when he felt there were no more worlds left to conquer. He died of a fever at the age of thirty-two in 324 BC. He left no heirs, and so his four generals divided his kingdom. Ptolemy took Egypt and Southern Syria. Antigonus claimed most of Northern Syria and West Babylon. Lysimachus held Thrace and Western Asia Minor. Finally, Cassander ruled Macedonia and Greece.[13]

Selucus I, in the battle of Ipaus in 301 BC, took the territories of Antigonus and Lysimachus. For many years, there were constant battles between the groups.

In 201–200 BC, Antichous III (also known as the Great) defeated Egypt and gained control of Palestine.

His attempts to Hellenize the Jews brought about the Maccabean revolt, which we will cover in the section on the Jewish state. Their rule in Syria ended in 63 BC when Pompey made Syria a province of Rome. It was their rule in Palestine that brought the Greek language to the Jews.

Before the Selecide rule, the Ptolemies of Egypt ruled over the Jews. The death of Cleopatra in 30 BC marked the last of the Ptolemies. Rome then made Egypt her granary. Alexandria had always been a place where the Jews could live. In Alexandria there was a great library founded to contain all the important works of the world. Under the Ptolemy Philadelphus (285-256 BC) the Jewish scriptures were translated into Greek. This was called the Septuagint Bible and was used by the New Testament writers.

The cultural effects of the Hellenistic kingdom were lasting. They introduced Greek customs and manners in the east. Their architecture prevailed. The Greek language became the language of the courts and common people.

The gospel of Christ, with a Greek Bible from which to preach and with the Greek language as its universal medium of communication, soon reached the outposts of civilization.[14]

The Jewish State

The Jews said to Jesus that they were not under bondage to anyone.[15] Nevertheless, the history of the nation reveals otherwise.

Babylonian Rule

Following the Jews' disobedience to God, the nation was taken away in exile. This began with the fall of Israel in 722 BC and was fully established with the conquest of Judah in 597 BC.

The nation went under Babylonian rule when Nebuchadnezzar overran Judea and captured Jerusalem. This is officially when the independent Jewish state ended. Mattaniah was renamed Zedekiah and placed as a puppet king, and the nation had a twilight existence from 597 to 586 BC. In 590 BC, Zedekiah thought he was powerful enough to rebel against Babylon, and he cast his lot with Egypt. Nebuchadnezzar did not overlook the challenge, and in 586 BC, he leveled the walls of Jerusalem and deported the population to Babylon.

The end of the Jewish state did not end Judaism. What we recognize as "orthodox Judaism" began here. During this captivity, synagogue worship began (because of the loss of the Temple), and the study of the Law replaced the sacrifices while they were captive.

Persian Rule

Cyrus, king of Persia, captured Babylon by diverting the Euphrates River in its flow. As the leader of the Persians, Cyrus was a benevolent despot. It was Cyrus who decreed that the Jews could return to their homeland. He even helped to rebuild the Temple from the Royal Treasury.

Not all the Jews returned. About 42,000 from Judah, Benjamin, and Levi did—and they arrived in Jerusalem in 537 BC. They began at this time to rebuild the Temple under Zerubbabel. Facing much opposition from the people of the land, however, they did not complete the rebuilding of the Temple.

For seventeen years, there was no further work on the Temple, until Haggai and Zechariah returned. Once again the local opposition raised its head, but this time a request was sent to Darius—who searched the records and decreed for the work to continue. The Temple was finished in 516 BC in time for the Passover observance.

From 516 to 458 BC, the records are silent. Then we have the record of Nehemiah returning, and in two months the walls and the city were intact. He also promoted social and economic reforms. Also during this time, Ezra promoted knowledge of the Law.

It was during the time of Nehemiah that Manasseh, the grandson of the high priest, was expelled to Mt. Gerizim where he established a rival cult. This became the center of the Samaritans.

During this seventy-year captivity period, two aspects of Jewish life disappeared: the monarchy and the prophets. The priesthood became more political during this time, and we find the beginning of the scribes. These were learned transcribers of the law, and they came to be held on the same plane as the priests themselves. We also find the Great Synagogue established. It was a council of 120 men, which later would evolve into the Sanhedrin of Jesus' day.

Ptolemies

During the years 322 to 198 BC, the Jews were under the heel of the Ptolemies. Comparatively little is known of this period. Under the first Ptolemies, many of the Jews were deported to Alexandria, but they appear to be a free community. The study of the Law and strict observance of the same was zealously maintained.

It was during this time that the younger Jews took on the manners and customs of the Greeks. During this time period, the Septuagint was created. Josephus speaks of a legend that says that seventy-two elders (six from each tribe) completed their work in seventy-two days, and when it was read, all the Jews approved it. This was the version of the Old Testament that Jesus and his disciples used.

Seleucidae

From 198 to 168 BC, the Jews were under the rule of the Seleucidae. The first ruler was Seleucus. He died in 175 BC, and his brother Antiochus IV came to rule. The people called him *Epimanes* (madman) instead of *Epiphanes* (Manifest God).

Antiochus became embroiled in a contest with Egypt and was defeated. He took his anger out on the Jews. On December 15, 168 BC, he set up an image of Zeus in the Jerusalem Temple and sacrificed a sow on the altar in the Temple. Judaism was forbidden at this time.

In the village of Modin, an old priest named Mattathias started a revolt against Antiochus and his forces. He was forced to flee into the wilderness region, and there he died. His successor in the revolt was a man named Judas, who would carry the nickname Maccabæus (the Hammer) because of the way that he fought.

Maccabbæan

From 168 to 142 BC, the Jews, under Maccabæus, routed the Seleucidae and recaptured Jerusalem. They cleansed the Temple and established a new feast—Hanukkah. Soon they had conquered all of Palestine. Throughout the fighting Judas had appealed to Rome, but no help came. Judas was killed in battle, and his brother Jonathan took command. The war drug on until 143 BC when Demetrius II of Syria granted Simon, another of the brothers, freedom.

Hasmonean Dynasty

Simon was then made high priest for life. This was a happy time for the Jews, but it was short lived. Demetrius was dethroned by the Parthians. War once again followed, and this time the Jews were victorious.

Ptolemy murdered Simon and two of his sons in 135 BC, John Hyrcanus (a son of Simon) took possession of Jerusalem before the Ptolemies could capture it. At the death of the Syrian ruler, Syria fell into civil war. John Hyrcanus went in and conquered Idumea and Samaria.

Hyrcanus was established as high priest and head of state, becoming the founder of the Hasmonean Dynasty. When he died, he left the dynasty to his wife and son Judah Aristobulus. Judah quickly imprisoned his mother and brothers to hold total rule. This did not last long, for Judah died shortly after coming to power.

There was constant unrest in the region until finally Hrycanus II cast his lot with Caesar. Hrycanus was made the head of the Jewish state. He appointed Antipater his minister to control the region. Antipater was granted Roman citizenship. He then appointed his son Phasel as the prefect of Jerusalem and his other son Herod the prefect of Galilee. Thus, the Hasmonean dynasty lasted from 142 to 37 BC.

Herodian Rule

From 37 BC on, the nation of Israel was under the rule of the Romans. We have covered this in a previous section. Here, let us view those kings who were directly in the Palestine region during the time of Christ.

Herod the Great - ruled from 37 to 4 BC. He was twenty-two at the beginning of his rule. During the invasion of the Parthians, he hid his family and escaped to Rome. By either smooth talk or secret intrigue, he was named king of the Jews.

His first act was to name a high priest. He named Aristobulus to this position, even though he was under age. Aristobulus was so well-liked that Herod became jealous. While throwing a feast in his honor in Jericho, Herod had the servants drown Aristobulus in a bathtub. Herod was sent to Egypt to answer for his crime but was released. He went to Rome for a conference with the Emperor Octavian. When he returned, he found his wife cold to him, and consequently had her executed. Remorse over this act caused him to fall physically and mentally ill.

Herod did not win the friendship of the Jews. His Idumean blood made him a foreigner. He used the priesthood as a political tool, and his lifestyle was loose and immoral. The last days of Herod were filled with violence and hatred. He murdered his sons. When at one point he appealed to Augustus for permission to execute his own son Antipater, Augustus replied that he would rather be Herod's *hus* (hog) than his *huios* (son).

Herod eventually died of cancer of the intestines, dropsy—and many believe—of a guilty conscious on April 1, 4 BC. The jealous and unscrupulous character of this man explains his treatment of the Wise Men and the slaying of the children in Bethlehem.[16]

Herod's will left his reign to Archelaus. Archelaus, Philip, and Antipas went to Rome fighting over the rulership of this region. The Jews also went to Rome begging for mercy at Augustus' court. The decree of Augustus set up the tetrarchy as follows:

- Archelaus–Judea, Samaria, Idumea.
- Antipas–Galilee and Perea.
- Philip–Batanea, Trachonitus, Aurantis.

Archalaus - ruled from 4 BC to 6 AD. He promoted the building of public works in his short reign. The Jews also disliked him. Finally, Augustus banished him to Gaul in 6 AD. The only reference to him in the New Testament is in Matthew 2:22.

Philip - ruled from 4 BC to 34 AD. He was the happy exception to the Herods. He followed their precedent in building, but was fair in his dealings with people. He was married to Salome, the daughter of Herodias.

The Jewish historian Josephus has nothing but good to say about this man. He is only mentioned in the New Testament in Luke 3:1.

He died peacefully in 34 AD. In 37 AD, his section of the tetrarchy was given to his nephew Agrippa I.

Herod Antipas - ruled from 4 BC to 39 AD. He is the most prominent Herod in the Gospels. Jesus refers to him as "that fox."[17] He built a capital city and named it Tiberius, but he had to colonize it by force because it was built on top of a graveyard. The Jews refused to enter it. His government was modeled on the pattern of the Greek governments.

Herod Antipas was a Jew by religion. He, therefore, was concerned with the Law. It was his marriage to Herodius that would cost him in many ways. It caused him to murder John the Baptist and eventually cost him his kingdom.

Herod Antipas was the Herod that Jesus was tried before in the Gospel accounts.

Herod Agrippa I - ruled from 37 to 44 AD. He was

the son of Aristobulus and Bernice, who were cousins. Bernice was the daughter of Salome, the sister of Herod the Great.

The Emperor Caligula gave him his appointment. He had enough sympathy for the Jews and influence in Rome to keep Caligula from erecting a statue of himself in the Temple at Jerusalem.

Agrippa was in Rome when Claudius came into power and was given all the territory that had originally been that of Herod the Great.

He himself lived in Jerusalem and worshipped in the Temple. He is one of the first persecutors of Christianity. He executed James, the leader of the Jerusalem Church, and imprisoned Peter with the intentions of executing him also.[18]

His death occurred suddenly in 44 AD.

Herod Agrippa II - ruled from 50 to 100 AD. He was the son of Agrippa I and was given from Rome the rights to rule. When Festus became Procurator of Judea, Agrippa II visited with him. Thus, Paul was tried before Herod Agrippa II.[19]

Although Agrippa II had a good knowledge of Judaism, he never had any convictions toward it. In the 66 AD revolution in Israel, he openly sided with Rome.

B. Social

In both Judaism and the pagan world there was a class system. There was a wealthy aristocracy and a large number of poor people.

In Judaism, the aristocracy was the priests and the rabbis. They were the ones who controlled all the business traffic connected with the Temple. This business was the sale of sacrificial animals and the exchanging of the Roman coinage into Temple money. Among the Sanhedrin were the affluent men of that day. Men like Nicodemus and Joseph of Arimathea were considered to have a firm financial base.

The majority of people in Judaism were poor. Joseph and Mary were in this lower class. The one redeeming quality of the social system in Judaism was that the social divisions were restrained by the Law. All were equal in God's sight.

Contrasted was the pagan society. The aristocracy was made up of the newly acquired landholders. They owned all the public lands and bought out the poor. They were a major discouragement to the poor. Because of these upper class people, the middle class had almost disappeared. The hungry, idle crowds of people would vote for any candidate running for Senate whose promises sounded better than their competitors.

The pagan world had a large number of plebs. These were the poor people, numerous and in a pitiful condition. They would follow anyone who had food and entertainment.

The largest segment of the pagan world was made up of slaves and criminals. Possibly one-half of the civilization was made up of men who were free. Of these, only a small segment were men with "full right" citizenship.[20] War, debt, and the birth rate were the cause of this large section of the population. While today we use machinery, in those days they used cheap labor. Slavery was a very debasing form of life. Trickery, flattery, and fraud were the slave's best tools.

Since the slaves were often the teachers of that day,

corruption was spread, as they would instruct their charges in how to do what they were doing.

Nowhere in the New Testament is slavery directly attacked or defended. Nevertheless, Christian influence weakened it.[21] This group of despairing and disinherited people became the fertile breeding ground for criminal activity.

The ghastly picture that Paul paints in Romans 1:18–32 was not overdrawn. There were no standards in paganism to check the downward drift.

Cultural Attainments

Under Augustus there was a literary revival. Vergil, Horace, and Ovid were the prophets of their age with their different brands of poetry and storytelling. Between the time of Augustus and Nero there was a lull in literature. Under Nero there arose the stoic philosopher Seneca, who wrote essays. The literature at this time took a turn toward self-criticism of the times.

In the realms of art and architecture, we find that construction was continual during the time of the Roman Empire. Mainly they produced utilitarian buildings. They used the arch for good effect. Bridges, aqueducts, and theatres still stand as monuments to their building skills.

The realm of music and drama was one of bad influence upon the people. These forms were committed to entertaining the mob, not to intellectual thought. Presentations were shameless, course, cheap, and full of moral degradation. They taught obscenity and lust.

Where the theatre taught obscenity and lust, the Arena glorified brutality. Bloody contests between men and beasts, or between men and men,[22] were promoted by the emperor.

They were not interested in science or math to any large extent. They were mainly interested in land measurement and calculating financial transactions. Geography was heavily studied. Medicine flourished during this time period.

Compulsory education was unknown at this time. Education was done in the house by the slaves. When there were private schools, they were dreary, with the curriculum being only reading, writing, and arithmetic. Greek and Latin were learned by rote memory. Public speaking was emphasized. Those who did well went to the Greek universities to study philosophy.

Jewish boys were somewhat the same. They learned to read and write from the Old Testament, and they were to learn large sections of the Old Testament by rote memory. They learned the traditions and rituals of their religion. A real scholar learned from a Rabbi such as Paul did under Gamaliel.[23]

Languages

There were four major languages used in that day. Latin was the language of the courts and the law system. Greek was the language of culture, used in writing and theatre. Aramaic was the chief language used in speaking and business. The Hebrew used in Palestine was a dead language by the time of Jesus and was not understood by most people. The wide use of Aramaic, Latin, and Greek is shown in the inscription placed over the cross of our Savior.[24]

The moral standards of the time of Jesus were low.

Only crime was news, any virtue around basically went unnoticed. Moralists like Seneca had lofty ideas and words, but they went basically unnoticed. Paganism was unable to lift itself out of its moral morass—this in turn brought about pessimism and depression. One is forced to ask, "Does this sound like today?" Are we copying the trends of the ancient Roman Empire?

In the previous chapter, we looked at the worlds of politics and society as they led up to, and were, in the days of Jesus and the disciples. In this chapter, let us finish our picture of the first century world by looking at the economical and religious aspects of this time period.

A. Economic

Judging by the ruins uncovered by archaeologists, we can see that the coastal territories were more fertile than they are today. Agriculture played an important part in the lives of those who settled the Canaanite regions. The Jews brought with them knowledge learned while slaves in Egypt. The major area was in the form of vine dressing. In Jesus' day you would find many gardens, which were vineyards. A good source of information on this topic can be found in Ralph Gower's book *The New Manners and Customs of Bible Times*. The student is encouraged to acquire this text and/or take a course in Bible times manners and customs.

In Jesus' day manufacturing was not important. Goods were produced by human labor. Any factories of that day were made up of slaves. The rule of the day was small shops. Every village had artisans and workers who produced what was needed. Any type of luxury good was imported from larger cities.

The major monetary unit in Jesus' day was the denarius.[25] About forty denarii made up the gold aureus or, as we know it, the pound. A denarius was the equivalent of a normal day's wage for a workingman. Therefore, we see the extent of the needed food to feed the five-thousand when they said it would take over two hundred penny-worth.[26] Banking was carried on to a point, but not as intricately as today. Money changing, the occupation of trading the Roman coinage for Temple coinage at a profit, was very prevalent. It was a thriving business that brought in much profit for those involved.

One important part of the economy in that day was the area of transportation. Roman roads by Jesus' day were the best in the world. They would excavate the topsoil, fill the area with three layers of road material, crown the center for drainage, and then pave them with stone. Some of these roads are still in use today. Vehicles in that day depended upon the wealth of the personage. The rich traveled by light carriage, while the poor walked. Others, who could afford them, would use donkeys and horses.

Inns of the day were at convenient distances for food and shelter. Few of these were luxurious, and fewer still were clean. They were filled often with vagabonds and rouges. The upper class would depend upon friends whenever they traveled.

Commercial transportation in that day was mainly by water. The merchant ships of the day were big, some over two-hundred feet long. They used sails but had oars for emergencies and when becalmed in the water. Paul, when he was shipwrecked, was aboard an Alexandrian merchant ship.[27] Warships of the day were lighter and faster. These were propelled by a galley of slaves using oars. This allowed for mobility and maneuverability.

B. Religious

There were two major divisions in the world as far as religion went in that day. The pagan world mainly followed the Graeca-Roman pantheon, while the chosen people of God followed the teaching of Judaism. We will study them in these divisions.

Graeca-Roman Pantheon

Christianity did not begin in a religious vacuum in which men were blankly waiting for something to believe. The original primitive Roman religion was that of animism. Animism is the belief that objects such as rocks, trees, wind, etc., are alive and have souls. They had a belief in the existence of demons and spirits. With this in mind, each farmer worshipped his own deity of nature.

When Rome conquered Greece, there began a fusion of Greek worship with that of Roman worship. They began to match up their respective deities. The Greek Zeus was Rome's Jupiter, the monarch of the sky. The Roman Neptune was the same as the Greek Poseidon, ruler of the sea. The Roman Pluto was the Greek Hades who controlled the underworld. By the time of Christ, much of this pantheon worship had diminished. People saw the gods as magnified men, and the gross immorality and petty squabbles of the gods brought them into ridicule by the satirists and philosophers of the day.

Up until the time of Rome, each city-state would worship its own personal deity. However, vanquished people tend to abandon faith in gods who are too weak or fickle to aid them. An example of this type of cult worship is found in Acts 19 with the worship of Artemis of Ephesus (also known as the goddess Diana).

The concentration of executive power in one man was unprecedented in history. The fact that he was able to utilize these powers for the good of the empire created the feeling that he must be divine. Thus, the Imperial cult did not grow up arbitrarily. It grew gradually as people looked more and more to the leader to supply and protect. It was during the time of the Emperor Domitian that there was a strong attempt to force the subjects to worship him. The Christians, in turn, refused to worship him, and this precipitated the violent persecution brought upon them.

Neither state nor emperor worship proved satisfying. Men were seeking a more personal faith that would bring them in contact with a deity, and they were ready for anything that would promise them that possibility. All of the mystery religions of that day centered on a god who had died and come back to life through rituals and incantations. No direct mention of these religions are made in the New Testament, unless it is Paul's reference to the "worship of angels" found in Colossians 2:18, 19.

There was a strong belief in magic in this time period. It was so widespread that Jew and Gentile both believed. Under the ruler Tiberius, horoscopes reached their peak of popularity. We find some references in the New Testament to the Jewish interest in the Occult. There is a reference to the Pharisees casting out demons.[28] In Ephesus, after the great conversion of the people in that city, they burned magic books valued at fifty-thousand pieces of silver.[29] Astrology was popular, and the Zodiac was heavily relied upon. The New Testament is openly hostile to the Occultic practices of the day.

When religion degenerates into empty ritualism or ignorant superstition, thoughtful men may abandon it for a lack of satisfaction. Philosophy is the attempt to correlate all existing knowledge about the universe into a systematic form and to integrate human experience with it. Philosophy does not depend upon God; it is a man-centered approach to life. There were seven main realms of philosophy in the day of Jesus, and we will quickly review them.

Platonism

This form of philosophy was founded by Plato. He was a student of Socrates. His major concept is that the real world is the world of ideas, and that the material world that we view is a shadow of reality. To Plato, knowledge is salvation and ignorance is sin. The problem with Platonism is that it is too abstract to gain the attention of the common person.

Gnosticism

This philosophy gains its name from the Greek word *Gnosis*, which means knowledge. This system promised salvation by knowledge. Matter was considered evil, and thus man gained salvation by renouncing the material world. The search that man needed to make was in the realm of the invisible world. Many of the New Testament books and much of the New Testament apologetics were dealing with the topic of Gnosticism. Gnosticism brought about two logical conclusions—that of asceticism, or that of full physical gratification.

Neo-Platonism

This was the teaching of Plato with the added Persian element of dualism. The spirit was considered good, while the material, or body, was considered evil. Death brought about the true spiritual life of the individual. The Neo-Platonists could not accept the union of God and man, thus to them, the idea of the resurrection was unthinkable.

Epicureanism

This philosophy was named for Epicurius of Athens. They believed that the world was started by a shower of atoms. Some of these atoms collided, and caused others to collide. Soon more collisions occurred, and from those random collisions, the universe came forth. Thus they believed in a world of chance. There is no purpose or design; there are no absolute standards or good. The highest level anyone can achieve is the absence of pain. It was essentially a very anti-religious philosophy. It brushed aside all concepts of sin. It became very popular because it did not indulge in abstracts as the other philosophies did.

Stoicism

This worldview was founded by Zenos of Cyprus. They did not recognize a God; they believed that the universe was ruled by absolute reason. Thus conformity to reason became the highest good. Perfect self-control is the goal of a Stoic. The universe is to be accepted, not changed. They were, therefore, extremely fatalistic in their approach to life. They had very high moral standards—but each man was responsible for himself and to himself.

Cynicism

This worldview grew out of Socratic teaching. To the cynic, the height of virtue was to have no wants. Often they would be vulgar and indecent just to show they were different. They dealt in a false brand of humility.

Skepticism

If knowledge rests upon experience, then there is no final standard. There is no such idea as truth—thus say the Skeptics. This line of thinking will end with complete mental paralysis.

Cynicism and Skepticism arose from the abandonment of standards. Cynicism arose with the abandonment of ethics, and Skepticism with the abandonment of intellectual standards.

However popular these and other variant philosophies were, they were unsatisfactory because they were too abstract for the ordinary man to grasp in their entirety. They also lacked a finality, their reasoning always ended with a "peradventure." Thus, philosophy in contrast to its own name was not successful in the quest for truth.

In contrast to the emptiness and vagueness of the Pagan Religious systems, we find the people of the Book—Judaism.

Judaism

Among the religions of the Roman Empire, Judaism was unique. It was made up of nationals, but it had proselytes by the hundreds. It is exclusively monotheistic, based upon a direct revelation from God. Christianity is a child of Judaism, having its beginnings and roots in the teachings of the Old Testament. All of the authors of the New Testament except Luke were Jews. Christians were first known as a sect of the Nazarenes—a branch of Judaism. In addition, of course, we must remember that our Savior Jesus was a Jew by birth.

The Judaism that was in existence at Christ's birth was largely a result of the exile. Prior to the exile, the nation had been surrounded by powerful wealthy heathen nations, and the Jews were constantly leaving the instructions of God to follow these other nations. They needed to make a decision—either follow God or be dispersed into the nations. The exile woke up the nation to the extreme to which they had gone.

Captivity changed the form of Judaism. Now they enforced the ban on idols. Their bitter lesson taught them to look only to God. The enforced cessation of sacrifice brought in the study of the Law, or Torah, as the central point. Scribes who studied and interpreted the Law became as important as the priests did. Without the Temple, they needed a new center of worship. Thus, the synagogue evolved. Even after the Temple was rebuilt, the synagogue remained in importance. Wherever there were ten Jewish men, they established a synagogue. There is no mention of this method of worship in the Old Testament, but they flourished in the New Testament times. Some of these changes were inevitable, but in the main, Judaism retained the essential principles of worship as prescribed by the Law and preached by the prophets.

Central to the faith of Judaism was the teaching of one God—monotheism. Deuteronomy 6:4, the Shema, was the declaration of the Jew. God was often viewed as eternal, superior to all, impersonal. Christianity would present God as real, personal, and knowable.

To the Jew, man was endowed with the ability to choose either good or evil. He could choose, in turn, life or death. The Law was what summarized the whole duty of man to God, and it was how a man established his relationship with God. Sin to the Jew was a wrong relationship to the revealed Law of God. Prior to the exile, rewards and punishment were viewed as connected to the nation as a whole. During the exile, this view began to move to an individual accountability before God.

Dealing with the area of rewards and punishment opened the question of life hereafter. Sheol is alluded to, the idea of the resurrection appears in the poetical books and the later prophets, but the Old Testament dealt mainly with the habitation of the Jews in Palestine. Their Messianic expectations were of a political deliverer, they looked for a warrior king—overlooking the prophecies of God's suffering servant in the Scriptures.

Temple

The original Temple was built by Solomon as told in the Old Testament. It was destroyed in 586 BC by the troops of Nebuchadnezzar. A second Temple was started in 537 BC and completed in 516 BC. Less than four hundred years later in 168 BC, Antiochus plundered this Temple and set up an altar to Zeus in it. This set off the Maccabæan revolt led by Judas Maccabæus, who cleansed and repaired the Temple. This Temple was still standing in 63 BC when Pompey conquered Jerusalem.

In 54 BC it was robbed of its treasures, and when Herod took the city, part of it was burned in 37 BC. During Herod's reign, he undertook the rebuilding of the Temple. It was completed in 64 AD, just a few short years before it was destroyed.

The Temple of Herod was a building of white marble. A large part of it was covered in gold, which reflected the sunlight and made it a dazzling splendor to behold. In the Temple proper, there was the Holy Place. In this was housed the Table of Shewbread on the north, the Minorah on the south, and the Altar of incense in between. Only the priests were allowed to enter the Holy Place. Behind the Holy Place was the Most Holy Place (Holy of Holies). It is believed to have been empty in Jesus' day with possibly the Ark of the Covenant destroyed.[30] The High Priest would enter the Most Holy Place once a year to make atonement with the shed blood of the sacrificial lamb.

The division between the Holy Place and the Most Holy Place was a double heavy veil. This is recorded as having rent from the top to bottom in the gospel accounts.[31]

The court of the Priests housed the Altar of Burnt sacrifice. Here a perpetual fire was kept burning. The Temple was the religious and political center of Judaism.

Synagogue

The synagogue played a large part in the growth and persistence of Judaism. In the synagogue the study of the Law took the place of the ritual sacrifice, the rabbi replaced the priest, and the communal faith was applied to daily life.

Each synagogue had a leader, possibly elected by a vote of the members. This attendant, or Hazzan, acted as custodian and was responsible for all the property of the synagogue. Occasionally, he was also the schoolmaster.

By Jesus' day, the buildings were substantial, built of stone, and their furnishings depended upon the local wealth. All synagogues had a chest, the scrolls, a platform for the reading desk, lamps, and benches.

The standard synagogue service began with the Shema, reciting of Deuteronomy 6:4 and 5. Following this was the Berakot, or reading of the Blessings. This was followed by ritual prayer and silent prayer. Then came the reading of the Scriptures. The Pentateuch (the first five

Books of Moses) was divided into 154 lessons. Those Jews in Palestine would cover these lessons in a three-year time span. They would also use the prophets in their time of reading. Following the reading was the sermon, which explained that which was read. The service then closed with the blessing pronounced upon the congregation.

As we can see, the influence of the synagogue and the order of service followed into the early Church. At first the Christians met in synagogues, but the total rejection of the Gospel by the Jews made the Church and synagogue part company.

Sacred Year

The Jewish year consisted of twelve lunar months with an intercalary month added when needed to equate the lunar year with the solar year. They had two different calendars—one for the Religious year and one for the Civil year. The Civil year started in the seventh month of the Religious calendar.

The life of the Jew revolved around seven feasts that are established in the Old Testament Law. These feasts are Passover, Pentecost, Rosh Hashanah, the Day of Atonement, Tabernacles, Lights, and Purim. Each has an important lesson for both the Jew and Christian alike.

Passover - The most important historically and religiously. This is the anniversary of the deliverance of the nation from Egypt. On this day every male Jew was to appear in Jerusalem. It is a picture of the work of Christ as our sacrifice.

Pentecost - The feast of weeks. This was the day of the first fruits. It took place seven weeks after Passover. Pentecost means fifty days. It is the anniversary of the giving of the law on Mount Sinai. To the Christian, it is the anniversary of the giving of the Holy Spirit power to the young Church.

Rosh Hashanah - The feast of trumpets. This was New Years Day for the Jews. It was the beginning of the Civil year. During the entire day, trumpets were blown in the Temple. To the Christian it is a reminder of the Trump of God blown to call us to meet Christ in the air during the rapture.

The Day of Atonement - This was a day of fasting for the Jew. The annual atonement was made this day by the High Priest. There was much of the symbolism of this day applied to Christ in the book of Hebrews. It is symbolic of the Tribulation.

Tabernacles - Five days after the Day of Atonement. This symbolized their wandering in the wilderness. This is a time of thanksgiving at the close of the harvest. A reminder of the time of the Millennium.

Hanukkah - Celebrated for eight days. This feast was established in 164 BC when Judas Maccabæus cleansed the Temple that was profaned by Antiochus Epiphanes. The Temple was rededicated to the service of God at this time. There is an account of a miracle of the oil used in this service.

Purim - Also called Lots. There was a minimum of religious observance; it was more of a national holiday, like our Fourth of July. Background for this can be found in the book of Esther.

The following is a compilation of the Jewish calendar to help put the times and feasts into perspective.[32]

Jewish Calendar

MONTH	APROXIMATE MONTH	SPECIAL DAYS
Nisan	April	14 - Passover 15 - Unleavened Bread 21 - Close of Passover
Iyar	May	
Sivan	June	6 - Feast of Pentecost-seven weeks from Passover (Anniversary of the giving of the law on Mount Sinai.)
Tammuz	July	
Ab	August	
Elul	September	
Tishri	October	1, 2 - Feast of Trumpets Rosh Hashanah, the beginning of the civil year. 10 - Day of Atonement 15-21 - Feast of Tabernacles
Marchesvan	November	
Kislev	December	25 - Feast of Lights or Dedication- Hanukkah
Tebeth	January	
Shebeth	February	
Adar	March	14 - Feast of Purim

Education

Education was important to the Jew in Jesus' day. It was limited, but thorough. Education was provided for boys only, with the ratio being usually about twenty-five boys per teacher. Girls were trained at home in preparation for marriage. Usually, the teacher sat on a small raised platform with the students at his feet. Thus, we see the statement in the New Testament "learning at the feet of..."[33]

Education was narrow but precise. They learned by rote and were taught to repeat exactly what was said. It was thoroughly integrated with theology.

Vocational education was necessary. "Whosoever does not teach his son a trade makes him a thief."[34] So, we see even Jesus was trained as a carpenter, and Paul was a tentmaker.

Literature

The Jews were the people of a book. The Old Testament to them was the voice of God. They learned it by memory and quoted freely from it. It was the basis of their lives.

They also had the Talmud. This was a collection of traditions with comments by the rabbis. It was made up of two parts, the Mishna and the Gemara; these were the oral Law. The name Talmud comes from the Hebrew word Lammid, which means "to teach." It has sixty-three sections in it, each dealing with some aspect of the law. To this day, the Talmud is the standard of Orthodox Judaism to regulate their faith and practice.

Sects

Pharisees - Their name means Separatists. They were the religious conservatives of their day. They originated shortly after the time of the Maccabees (approximately 135 BC). Their theology is founded upon the entire Old Testament. They attached great value to the oral traditions and followed them closely. The Pharisees believed in angels, spirits, immortality, and the resurrection of the body. They practiced rituals, fasting, tithing, and the keeping of the Sabbath. When you consider their beliefs and standards, you see that Jesus was a Pharisee in the purest sense. Today they are the orthodox Jews.

Sadducees - They were the liberals of their day. They were made up mainly of the Priestly class and were highly political. They were less numerous than the Pharisees but were the governing body of the day. They were corrupt politically. They adhered to the Torah only, refused the oral traditions, and were anti-supernaturalists.

Essenes - Their name possibly comes from the Greek *Hosios*, meaning Holy. They were an ascetic brotherhood with strict regulations to which they had to adhere. They had their property in common and worked for self-support. They were much like the Pharisees in their theology. You might picture them like the Christian monasteries of the Reformation times. They are never mentioned in the Gospels at all. But, we are aware of them, because the Dead Sea scrolls came from a community of Essenes located at Qumram.

Zealots - These were the political fanatics. They were a group of fanatical nationalists who advocated violence as a means of liberation from the Roman government. Simon Zelotes, one of Jesus' disciples, was a member of this sect.

Hebraists - Following the dispersion of the Jews, two groups evolved within those dispersed. The Hebraists were those who were firm Hebrews. They retained the religious faith along with the customs and language of their home. Paul was one of these.

Hellenists - The other group was the Hellenists. They had absorbed the Greek and Roman cultures. They spoke Greek and followed many of the Greek customs. They are mentioned in Acts 6, where the division between the Hebraists and Hellenists began to endanger the Church.

From all of this background God stepped into human history in human flesh and changed the course of events. As we continue now into the Books of the New Testament themselves, we can see where the writers are coming from, as well as where they are going.

The beginning of our study will start with the four biographies given of Jesus Christ. When we consider the fact that Jesus is the Son of God and that He maintains all the attributes of the Godhead, we see that these four biographies cannot in any way cover all there is to know about Him. In fact, John says at the end of his biography, "And there are also many other things which Jesus did, the which, if they should be written every one, I suppose that even the world itself could not contain the books that should be written. Amen."[35]

God saw that the important information was preserved for us in a manner that is indisputable. Some ask, "Why are there four accounts? Wouldn't one have sufficed?" In addition, the answer is simple. In the court of law, a judge or jury looks for more than one witness to an event. These four witnesses attest to the truthfulness of what we read.

Some ask, "Why do they differ in some of the minor details?" This also attests to the veracity of the accounts. If a judge hears all the witnesses saying exactly the same thing, he knows that there is collusion. I would recommend that the student purchase a good Harmony of the Gospels to read and see the order and correspondence of these accounts.

God chose four men of different backgrounds and different styles to record the message that the entire world might believe in Jesus.

As you study these different accounts, look to find the major thrust of the book. Matthew portrays Jesus as a king, Mark shows Him as the servant, Luke displays the humanity of Christ, and John blazes forth the glory of His Deity. As we read with this in mind, we better understand why the writers chose the miracles, parables, and accounts in their respective books.

Speaking of the miracles and parables, we must be reminded that Jesus did these not to entertain or draw crowds, but to teach vital lessons. As we observe the miracles and parables, look for these lessons. Let us now look at each of these books individually.

A. Matthew

The human author of this biography is the man Matthew. He goes by two names in the Bible—Matthew and Levi.[36] His names mean: Matthew–Gift of Jah; and Levi–To twine or unite. These point to the possibility that he had been born and raised in a religious Jewish home. His father is called Alphaues.[37] Matthew held the unpopular post of tax collector in Capernaum. Being a tax collector meant that he had sided with the Roman government, thus to other Jews he was a traitor and worse than a dog. He apparently was very wealthy, because this post was one that controlled the trade routes through the area. Every caravan passed by Matthew, and he would get Rome's share (and his own) from them, if they wished to continue on their way. He was personally called by Jesus[38] and responded quickly, leaving all that he had acquired. The first action we read following his reception of Jesus was to host a large party in honor of Jesus so that his friends could meet the Master also.[39] He faithfully followed and served the Lord while He was on earth. The last mention that we have of Matthew occurs in Acts 1:13, after which he disappears from church history.

When we try to place the date and place of the writing of this biography, we must seek for just possibilities. It is doubtful that it was written after the overthrow of Jerusalem in 70 AD, because there is no reference to fulfilled prophesies—especially in the Mount Olivet discourse in chapter 24. In addition, it was probably not written before the dispersion of the Jerusalem Christians in Acts 8:4, because there would be no need to write the events with which all were directly familiar. This makes the dates of writing at about 50 to 70 AD, or about twenty to forty years after the crucifixion. As to the location of the writing of this book, turning to outside sources it appears that this was a favorite book of the Christians in the region of Antioch—possibly because they knew the author firsthand. Therefore, it may be that the location of writing was Antioch.[40]

When we look at the book, we see that Matthew wrote in a topical fashion. He took themes and put the material together around these themes. Examples are the Beatitudes in chapters 5, 6, and 7, Parables in chapter 13, and a discourse on Eschatology in chapter 24. It is not surprising that Matthew would arrange the book in this fashion, seeing that he was an accountant by trade. These blocks of teaching are put together to teach us more about the Kingdom.

That brings in another point. Matthew is writing primarily to Jews to emphasize to them that Jesus is the fulfillment of the prophesy of the coming King of David. By portraying Jesus as a king, he wants his readers to see that Jesus is the Messiah—the promised one.

There are then five special considerations in this biography:

1. Matthew sought to prove to the Jews that Jesus was the Messiah. (Matthew 1:17)
2. Matthew had a special interest in the Church. This is the only account to mention the word "Church." (Matthew 16:18)
3. Matthew had a strong interest in Eschatology. (Matthew 24)
4. Matthew had a great interest in the teachings of the kingdom. (Matthew 4:23; 13:24, 31, 33, 44, 45, 47)
5. Matthew wrote to show Jesus as the King. (Matthew 27:37)

B. Mark

The second of the four biographies that we have was written by a man named John Mark. He carries a Hebrew and a Roman name. Possibly he was from a mixed marriage. John is from the Hebrew word that means "God is gracious," and Mark is from the Latin name that means "warlike one."

He was an understudy or assistant to Paul, Barnabus, and to Peter. He is possibly ten years younger than any of the apostles. We know that he is the son of a woman named Mary, who is mentioned in Acts 12:12. Her home where the prayer meeting for Peter was held. Some even believe that this may have been where the "upper room" used during the last supper was located. Some believe that he may have been at the arrest of Jesus. They take this from his account in chapter 14:51, 52 about a young man hidden in the bushes. They believe that this may have been Mark.

He was a cousin to Barnabus and by this was able to leave with Barnabus and Saul on the first missionary journey.[41] Mark left after their stop on Cyprus,[42] which later caused a rift between Barnabus and Paul. He disappears from the records until later when Paul finds him useful.[43]

It is believed that he wrote from the teaching of Peter. When we consider that Matthew and John were Apostles, Luke was a confidant and friend of Paul—we see that Mark needed to be tied in firsthand to be accepted. This may have come from the Apostle Peter's recollections, sermons, and teachings.

Researching the date and place, we again see that this must have been written before the destruction of Jerusalem in 70 AD, most scholars place it in the early 60s, somewhere between 55 to 65 AD. Some believe that this may have been the first written account. The place suggested for the writing is Rome. The style is such as a Roman mind would think. It is terse, clear, and pointed. He uses many Latin terms in his writing, and there is little emphasis on Jewish laws and customs.

Writing from Rome to the Roman Gentiles, we see Mark as a book of action. It is brief, pictorial, curt, clear cut, and forceful. It is like a series of snapshots. As Matthew wrote topically, Mark appears to write chronologically. Many of the Harmony studies are based on Mark. He consistently portrays Jesus as moving toward a goal. He aims at being a book of vividness and attains this very well.

Mark portrays Jesus as a servant. The key verse in this book is Mark 10:45, and it sums up his message very well. Jesus is a servant moving on a mission—moving toward accomplishing what he was sent to do. At the same time,

Mark appears to write evangelistically, seeking to bring the person and work of Christ before the public.

The shortest and the simplest of the four, Mark gives a crisp and fast moving look at the life of Christ. With few comments, he allows Christ's life to speak for itself.

C. Luke

The third of the biographers was different from the rest. He was a Gentile. His name was Dr. Luke. He is not mentioned in the book, and the reader must go to the book of Acts to ascertain the author's name. Little is known of Luke. He was well educated and of a high literary ability. He was a keen observer and tended to write from a physician's point of view.[44]

Placing this book is difficult. If he wrote this during Paul's imprisonment, it was then written from Rome. When dating it we see that it was written before the Book of Acts, but it had to be written after Christianity had become large enough to attract Gentile attention and inquiry. The period for this book is between 55 and 65 AD.

Luke writes historically. He makes a point that he is very careful about the details of what he is writing.[45] He wrote to the Gentiles and more specifically to one named Theophilus, a Greek who may have been a convert or one that Luke wanted to convert. He wrote to portray Jesus as a Man. He shows forth His humanity as well as His Godhood. He pictures Christ as the perfect Son of Man empowered by the Holy Spirit. Luke wants his readers to see that Jesus is the fulfillment of the Greek ideal of human perfection.

Luke gives the most complete account of the ancestry

of Christ. He also goes into detail about the birth of Jesus and is the only one who mentions anything about his childhood. Now would be a good time to point out to the student that only Matthew and Luke give the accounts of the background and birth of Jesus. There is a logical reason for this if one stops to consider the purposes for writing. Matthew portrays Him as a King—the reader would like to know what credentials He has that give Him this title. Luke shows His humanity—this is enhanced by the accounts of His birth and childhood. Mark writes about a servant, and very few people care about the ancestry of a slave. John shows that Jesus is God—and that He has no beginning.

The main emphasis that Luke takes is one of doctrine. The doctrine of Soteriology (salvation) is prominent in this account. The key verse Luke 19:10 emphasizes that salvation is prominent. If one was to set a simple outline to the book of Luke, it might be like this: Chapters 1:1–19:27=Seeking the Lost. Chapters 19:28–24:53=Saving the Lost. The doctrine of Pneumatology (Holy Spirit) is also important. We see a number of people who are empowered by the Holy Spirit.

D. John

The last of the biographers of Jesus Christ is a man named John. From the book we can draw certain facts. First, he was a Jew who was accustomed to thinking in the Aramaic language. In addition, he was familiar with the Jewish traditions and feasts, which he takes time to explain. Finally, he was a Palestinian Jew—familiar with the territory that he is writing about. He never names himself in the book, but he is apparently very familiar to his readers. John, with his brother James, was partner in a fishing business, possibly with Simon and his brother Andrew. Jesus uses a nickname for James and John—"sons of thunder."[46]

By this, we can assume that they had an intense nature. John apparently had a temper that would erupt like a summer thunderstorm—violent and loud. He was the disciple who wanted to call down the wrath of God on the Samaritans[47]—later to be called the Disciple of Love.[48] John is a beautiful example of a man who could have been and was a great sinner, out of whom Christ made a great witness.

This is the latest of the four accounts. By all reckonings, John was written sometime between 90 and 100 AD. The consensus seems to be that he wrote this book from the city of Ephesus, where he possibly had been the pastor of the local Church for a long period.

His book was written to the whole world—Jew and Gentile alike. He portrayed Jesus as we have already pointed out to be God. Two important aspects of this work stand out. First, John wrote about what the others had left out. Possibly he had read the writings of Matthew, Mark, and Luke, and knew that there was more to be told. He covers the Judean ministry of Christ, while the other three had written almost entirely about His Galilean ministry. Most of the book of John is original in content. That is why scholars refer to the first three books as the Synoptic Gospels and this last one as the Johannine Gospel.

The second important aspect is that he wrote argumentatively. He wrote to combat a heresy that had spread quickly in the first century. This was the heresy of Gnosticism. The Gnostics separated the spiritual and the physical. To them, the physical was evil and the spirit was good. These two natures could not co-exist together. Thus, Jesus could not be man and God. If He was physical, He could not be God—and if He were God, He could not be physical. Thus John begins his biography with that glorious philosophical statement, "In the Beginning was the Word, and the Word was with God, and the Word was God… And the Word became flesh and dwelt among us…"[49]

In his book three words stand out as prominent. The words *signs*, *believe*, and *life*.[50] In the word *signs*, we find him giving us seven miracles that Jesus performs in areas where man cannot make changes. These range from the changing water into wine to the ultimate of raising Lazarus from the dead. All seven of the miracles in his book stress the Deity of Christ. The seven miracles are:

1. Changing water into wine, 2:1–11, the area of quality.
2. Healing of the Nobleman's son, 4:46–54, the area of space.
3. Healing of the impotent man, 5:1–9, the area of time.
4. Feeding of the 5000, 6:1–14, the area of quantity.
5. Walking on the water, 6:16–21, the area of natural laws.
6. Healing of the blind man, 9:1–12, the area of misfortune.
7. Raising of Lazarus, 11:1–46, the area of death.

The next word is *believe*. It is used over ninety-eight times in the book. The emphasis is that when the signs convince us, we should believe and move on to a settled faith. The last word is *life*. John uses it to mean the sum total of all that is imparted unto the believer by his faith in Jesus. The book is therefore set up in a logical organization—in the signs is the revelation of God; in belief is the reaction that the signs are designed to produce; in life is the result that belief brings to the individual.

One last point, the biography of Jesus has a clear emphasis on the seven "I Ams" of Jesus. The use of "I Am" stresses the Deity of Jesus. The Jews of His day recognized this and sought for ways to kill Him for it. The seven "I Ams" are:

1. I am the Bread of Life–6:35
2. I am the Light of the World–8:12; 9:5
3. I am the Door (of the sheepfold)–10:7
4. I am the Good Shepherd–10:11, 14
5. I am the Resurrection and the Life–11:25
6. I am the Way, the Truth, and the Life–14:6
7. I am the True Vine–15:1

Four different men used by God to record the biography of His Son. Truth established in the mouth of four witnesses. Now He has established His Church. When He goes to the right hand of the Father, what will become of it? We will see as we look at the book of Acts—the book of Transition.

We now come to the book of Acts. The Bible gives the title as The Acts of the Apostles, though many believe that the book should be called the Acts of the Holy Spirit. As we study this book, we need to see the importance of what God is doing. This book is generally listed as a history book, and to a point it is, but it is more a revealing of the transitions that took place in that first century Church.

The Church was in existence at the beginning of the book of Acts. Jesus had started the Church when He called out His first followers. The word *church* is from the Greek word *ecclesia*, and means a "called-out assembly." The purpose for which this assembly is called out determines the kind of assembly that it is. In the New Testament, every assembly mentioned was a local, visible congregation of people. When one speaks of the home, meaning any home or each home, one is not speaking of one big, universal, invisible home. In the same manner, when the Bible speaks of Church, it is speaking of a local visible group of people.[51]

As was stated, Jesus began the New Testament Church when He called Simon, Andrew, James, and John to walk with Him beside the Sea of Galilee. Acts gives us the information of how this sect of Judaism transitioned into the worldwide outreach of today. Acts gives us a brief compact history of the work of God in the first century personalities, while omitting many others who also did much to further the kingdom here on earth. In chapters 1–

5, we find the record focusing upon Peter. The focus shifts in chapters 6 and 7 to the man Stephen, and it broadens a little and shows us the work of Barnabus, Philip, and Saul in chapters 8–12, finishing with the emphasis on Paul in the remaining chapters 13–28.

Acts is God disclosing to us how He transitioned that early group from a Jewish sect to a group of churches that was made up of all nationalities. It also shows us the transition from the physical presence of Jesus in His Church, leading and guiding, to that of the Holy Spirit leading and guiding the work.

The author of this work is Dr. Luke. He is continuing his thesis to Theophilus about what is happening in the movement of God. The Gospel of Luke gives the biography of Jesus, while Acts shows how the local Church that Jesus started became the many local churches of that first century. Luke probably wrote this during Paul's two-year imprisonment, making the date at about 61 AD. In all probability, it was written from Rome.

Jesus, when He ascended into heaven, had given that first Church what we call today the Great Commission, the task of evangelizing the world. Go tell, baptize, and teach the entire world He had said. But how? This was a small group by any comparison. In Acts 1:8, He gave them their marching orders. Reaching Jerusalem, Judea, followed by Samaria, then on to the whole world. As the group and number of churches would increase, they would be able to reach more and more of the world.

Luke, in turn, uses this as an outline for the treatise that he writes to Theophilus. Chapters 1:1 through 8:3 cover the Jerusalem/Judea work of the Church. Chapter

8:4 through 11:18 moves into the Samaritan region, and chapters 11:19 through 28:31 shifts to the whole world.

Luke was very careful in all that he records. He personally observed much of what he writes, but he also employs many eyewitnesses. We find information carefully collected from Paul, Barnabus, Timothy, and others. Luke wants to record for Theophilus a carefully compiled treatise on the first century move of God in His churches.

We will now go through the book of Acts in a quick tour.[52]

The account begins at the ascension of Jesus and records His last words of instruction to His disciples. The group then returned into Jerusalem where they stayed in the Upper Room seeking God for direction. Ten days after the ascension of Jesus, a major event took place, which established the Church for the work given to it.

A. Pentecost

Pentecost was a Jewish feast that took place fifty days after Passover. The Old Testament Jew saw this celebration as a remembrance—it was the anniversary of the giving of the Law on Mount Sinai. Here God changes the importance of this day for the fledgling Church. It now becomes the anniversary of the empowering of the Church by the Holy Spirit to perform the task given it by Jesus.

Some much-disputed signs accompanied this empowering. First, Acts 2:3 states that there was a sound as the sound of a mighty rushing wind. This author believes that, as we look in the Bible for clarification, a possible explanation of the meaning of this event is that it shows the presence of the Holy Spirit. We must remember that these are Jews who make up the first Church. Therefore,

God will use Jewish symbols to teach them the truths that they need. Jesus, when He taught the Rabbi Nicodemus, compared the Holy Spirit to the wind because to the Jew, this would bring to mind the picture that God paints in Ezekiel 37. In this great Old Testament chapter the wind is a picture of the Holy Spirit of God as He revives and restores the people of Israel. On this day of Pentecost, the wind would stir the memories of these Jews to the presence of the Holy Spirit.

Then, there were the split tongues of fire that settled on each of the people in the room. In the Old Testament, both the Tabernacle and the Temple (before Ezekiel) had the Shekina glory of God setting upon the Holy of Holies. This glory was displayed as a pillar of smoke and fire. These tongues of flame may have symbolized and assured the people of the way that they now had the Holy Spirit in them. Later, Paul will make reference that our bodies are the Temple of God.[53]

Finally, there were the phenomena of the speaking in tongues. Due to the Pentecostal and Charismatic movements, many incorrect doctrinal ideas abound. One must remember that these were not ecstatic languages spoken that day. Acts 2 lists the languages that were spoken by the early Church members. In Acts 2, two words are used in this passage. The Greek word *glossa* means "the ability of speaking another known language"—in this case without the benefit of structured learning. The other term is *dialektos*, which means "dialect." Neither of these terms infers a miraculous heavenly language. This work does not have the space to devote to a complete study of this gift, but the student is encouraged to seek the truth about this misused charismata.

An important section often lost in the miraculous is the preaching of Peter on this day. This is the first record of a sermon we have. There are three important parts to this sermon, which characterized the preaching of the early Church. The first is a narration of the life of Jesus with an emphasis upon the resurrection of Jesus. The resurrection was a major point in all the preaching of the early Church. Next, we find a call to repentance and placing faith in Jesus. Today the message of repentance is often glossed over or forgotten in our churches. Finally, we need to see that the message was strongly scriptural in content. Peter found that the Scriptures were the central emphasis in his defense of the good news. Because of these parts, the Spirit moved, and three thousand souls were added to the kingdom and to the Church that day.

B. Moving in Transition

Following the day of Pentecost, Luke records many more events. Chapter 3 is an account of a lame man who is healed by Peter and John—with the resulting reactions of the crowds and religious leaders. Chapter 4 introduces the beginning of the persecution by the religious leaders. Prison became almost a major part of the life of these early Church leaders. We find in chapter 4 that when faced with persecution, they did not pray for it to be removed, but prayed that they would be stronger in their witness. God granted this prayer.

By Chapter 8 we find that the people had settled into an easiness in Jerusalem. God had given them directions, and it was time to advance. Therefore, by sending persecution into the Church in Jerusalem, we find the people scattered throughout the known world. The main ones who stay behind in the local Church in Jerusalem were the Apostles. In this chapter, we are also introduced to the persecutions of a man named Saul.

Being driven from Jerusalem, we follow a man named Philip who goes to the region of Samaria. The Samaritans were a mixed race—part Gentile and part Jew. They kept most of their pagan religion, but they added Jehovah to be sure. Philip's preaching to the Samaritans was a surprising action for a Jew. Jews thought of Samaritans as less than dogs. The response of his teaching was amazing—many renounced their superstitions and accepted Jesus. The response was so surprising that the Church at Jerusalem sent Peter and John to confirm the truth of the matter.

While Philip was ministering in Samaria, the Lord sent him down to the desert region where we have the account of the conversion of the Ethiopian Eunuch. The importance of this conversion is recorded to emphasize that racial and national prejudices do not have any place in the churches of Jesus, and that God is concerned with individuals. When the Church grows and works with the masses, it is often easy to lose sight of the individual—who are important to God.

C. Saul

The next episode we have recorded is the conversion of the persecutor Saul. Saul was born into a strict Hebrew family. His native city was Tarsus in Cilicia. In this city was a great university noted for its courses in philosophy and medicine. Saul was educated in Greek philosophy, Hebrew language, and Scriptures. At the age of twelve he went to Jerusalem to learn from the Rabbi Gamaliel.[54] As was true in all Jewish households, Saul was taught a trade.

He became a proficient tentmaker. By the time he came into manhood, he was working to be a leader in Judaism. He had become a member of the Sanhedrin by the time he appears in Acts.

The death of Stephen was a continual thorn in his mind. He alludes to this in his speech in the Castle of Antonia as an experience he could not forget.[55] The book of Acts in Chapter 9 goes into detail about his confrontation with Jesus and his conversion. Following his conversion, he went from Damascus into the wilderness of Arabia for a period of three years. From this he comes forth prepared by God to be the Apostle to the Gentiles.

D. Continuing in Transition

At this point, we have been taken by Luke through the work of God in Jerusalem/Judea and Samaria. Now, Luke is about to take us into the expansion of the work into the churches of the whole world. The movement of expansion has its roots in the establishment of the Church at Antioch in Syria. From this point the work of God will begin a spreading move into the Gentile cities of Galatia, Asia, Mysia, Achaia, and beyond.

The Church at Antioch becomes the mother of all Gentile churches. It was from this church that the true concept of missions began. This church virtually superseded Jerusalem as the home of Christian preaching and evangelism. It was here that the term "Christian" first came into being.

In Acts 13, we have recorded the beginning of the first official missionary tour. Barnabus and Saul, with a small company, left Antioch and went to the isle of Cyprus. From this isle, they turned north and went into Asia Minor. We trace the movement of this missionary team through the region of southern Galatia. Iconium, Lystra, and Derbe all are cities that housed New Testament churches began by this movement.

Nevertheless, with the inclusion of Gentiles into the sect, it was not surprising that a great controversy arose over this. The fifteenth chapter of Acts is devoted to this Council at Jerusalem, which dealt with the problem. The struggle was over legalism and liberty. The Judaizers wanted to put everyone under the Old Testament law. However, Peter and Paul both saw that God had released us from the restrictions of the Law. Legalism is putting something with the cross to achieve salvation, but it is also putting something with grace to stay saved. This first council wisely saw that God was dealing in grace and liberty—not works and the law. It was prior to this event that the books of James and Galatians were written dealing with this great controversy.

After this council, Paul and Barnabus returned to Antioch, where after a short period of time they went separate ways, taking two different mission teams out to serve God. Paul and Silas went by land and returned to the southern Galatian churches to encourage them and to see how they were faring. It was during this trip that Paul encountered Timothy—a young man who would be trained by the apostle to minister in the early churches.

Finding the churches well in the southern Galatian region, Paul then turned his attention to other fields. Following a series of closed doors and a vision, Paul's team moves into the Macedonian region. The cities of Philippi, Thessalonica, and Beroea are written about. Persecution seemed to follow Paul wherever he went. He was often forced to leave cities. Nevertheless, in the seventeenth chapter of Acts we find a group of people who exhibit the true picture of being a Bible student. The Berean brethren received the message of Paul, but they were careful to study the Scriptures to see if what Paul said was true.[56] All Christians should spend time in God's Word approving or disproving what they are taught.

From Beroea Paul went into the city of Athens. Athens was one of the wonders of the old world. Here the great philosophers of the day would gather. Paul's preaching so intrigued the Athenian philosophers that they invited him to Mar's Hill[57] to share his teaching with them. Here the Apostle Paul encountered something new. Everywhere that he had gone previous to this, he started either a revival or a riot. Here the Athenians just laughed and walked off. This confused Paul and caused him to draw back and reconsider his approach.[58] He left Athens and went from an intellectual city to one of the basest cities in the Roman Empire. Corinth was possibly the most wicked city of its day. To "corinthianize" someone or something was a euphemism for living the vilest form of life. It was here that the Temple of Aphrodite stood. This Temple lodged over one thousand priestesses who were nothing more than prostitutes. Paul stayed at Corinth for a year and a half. He managed to establish a growing flourishing Church—though this Church was laden with problems.

Paul left Corinth and went to Ephesus with Priscilla and Aquila. After a few short trips, he returned to Ephesus and helped turn this Church into a hub of mission activity. For two years Paul preached there virtually unhindered.

Paul begins to plan what he may have considered his

most important mission trip—a trip to the imperial city of Rome. A grand goal beckoned unto him. If he could reach Rome with the gospel, it would become the evangelistic hub to the entire known world—after all, "all roads lead to Rome." With true missionary statesmanship he lays out his course of action. He plans to return for a short visit to Jerusalem and then to set out for Rome. Paul does not see a sidetrack that God has for him. Yes, Paul will go to Rome, but in the timing and manner that God chooses.

E. Paul's Imprisonment

This last section of the book of Acts contains the account of Paul's imprisonment, trials, and his voyage to Rome. It almost reads like an anticlimax. When one reads this, he is left with a feeling of incompleteness. Instead of showing how the movement expanded into Rome or Spain, the account leaves you with Paul under the custody of Rome in his own hired house. It tells nothing of his hearing before the emperor or of his ministry after this or of his martyrdom. The story ends very abruptly.

The abruptness may be accounted for by assuming that the author wrote all that he knew. He ended right where they were at the time that he sent this letter to Theophilus. If he was seeking to bring Theophilus up to date on what was happening, he would want to get the letter off as soon as possible. Luke may have been writing to prove that Christianity had no political pretensions. It was not a subversive movement to overthrow Rome; it was a spiritual movement to overthrow Satan. The persecutions that had arisen came from the Jews on religious grounds. All accusations that Christianity was against Rome were categorically false.

When Paul arrives at Jerusalem, there is an immediate clash with the religious leaders, in spite of his attempts at pacification. Paul had undertaken a Nazarite vow and was on his way to the Temple to pay the vow. He was demonstrating that he had no aversion to keeping the law voluntarily. The Jews from Asia assumed he had brought his Gentile friends into the forbidden sanctuary, so they accused him publicly, which started a riot.

The riot was so intense that a Roman military tribune had to intervene with armed cohorts. When Paul was arrested and taken out, he asked if he could address the crowd. This they let him do. He spoke of his conversion, and they were fine, but when he made mention of the Gentiles, the mob was aroused to riot again.

Paul was taken into custody to be interrogated. In this process, two things are brought out—first, Paul is innocent of any political or criminal charges, and second, Paul was a Roman citizen.

Through a series of events, Paul is placed in protective custody for a period of four years. Two years he spends in Caesarea, where the leader Felix hoped to extract a bribe from him. When Festus takes the place of Felix, Paul realized that the Jews' hatred would not cease, so he appealed to Caesar. He was transferred to Rome, and that period of waiting took two years.

This period of enforced inactivity was not fruitless. Paul was allowed contact with the outside world during this whole time. He was not allowed to travel, but he had the liberty to teach and to write within the limits of his cell or house. The letters that he wrote at this time testify that the growth of the movement had not stopped because of Paul's imprisonment. The literature that he produced at this time was more solid and didactic than anything he had written up to this time, with the exception of the letter to Rome. In spite of the change in Paul's plans with the imprisonment, God still had a plan of sending him to Rome. God sent him to witness and work in Rome under the expenses of the Roman government. God does work in mysterious ways.

In this decade of expansion, the movement of churches had grown and become established in themselves and their mission outreach. The transition of a Jewish sect to a Gentile world outreach had become firm. The transition from Jesus' bodily presence to the Holy Spirit's guidance had come to fulfillment.

Local Church Correspondence

The main section of the New Testament is made up of correspondence to individuals and local churches. These letters give us a full understanding of the operation of the local Church, pastoral responsibilities, and individual interactions as brothers and sisters in Christ. There are twenty-one letters recorded in the Bible. Obviously, these were not all the letters written, just the ones selected and inspired by God for our edification. In this section we will survey ten of Paul's letters. Nine are written to local churches, and one is to a personal friend. The remaining eleven letters will be studied in Chapters 7 and 8.

A. Romans

The letter to the Church at Rome is possibly one of the finest examples of combining doctrine and missionary purpose that we retain. This letter could well be an example of what Paul would do when he established new converts in churches.

In preparation for coming to the Church at Rome, Paul took time to write them this letter. Tradition places him writing it from the city of Corinth,[59] while some believe that he wrote it from Philippi—just prior to his sailing to Troas.[60] Paul appears to have many friends at Rome, and he states that he had tried frequently to visit them but had always been hindered.[61]

The Church at Rome was not a large one at this time, and it was made up mainly of Gentiles. The origin of the Church at Rome is uncertain. There were present on the day of Pentecost "strangers from Rome," who may have returned with the message of Christ. We know that Priscilla and Aquila had come from Rome and, according to Romans 16:3, had returned there. Any and all of these may have been the instrument used by God to establish a local Church in Rome. The traditional view held by the Catholic Church that Peter had founded the Church at Rome has no scriptural basis found in the New Testament.

Paul possibly had several reasons for wanting to go to Rome. He may have had a personal desire to see the Imperial City of which he held earthly citizenship. He perhaps had heard of the need for instruction in the faith for the believers in Rome. As always, he had a wish to forestall any activity of Judaizers in a group of certain importance in the Empire. Paul may have been looking to go from here into Spain, and he was hoping for their support. Paul no doubt also saw the factor that Rome would be a great center for all missionary activity—for it was said, "All roads lead to Rome."

This letter is devoted to the teaching of the truth. Most of the Pauline Epistles were written to deal with controversies or as corrections of problems in that local Church. This letter is strongly didactic. It is purely from the instructional point of view, presenting us with a fine example to be studied of first century apologetics.

Romans has been classed as the finest example that we have of a first century legal brief. It is as if Paul is arguing his case in the courtroom.[62] We can see the case being very carefully built up until a verdict is declared—"For all have sinned . . ." Humanity is guilty before a righteous and holy God.

The central theme of Romans is the revelation of the righteousness of God to man and its application to his spiritual need. Paul goes to great length to establish the theme as basic to all men, because a man cannot do business with God until a proper approach has been established. Even though the letter is directed to the Gentiles at Rome, it avows that salvation is universal in its scope.

The letter of Romans has long been the mainstay of Christian theology. Most of the technical terms we use today come form the pages of this treatise. Terms such as Justification, Imputation, Adoption, and Sanctification are all drawn from the vocabulary of this letter.

The structure of this letter provides a backbone to Christian thought. Paul works through the apologetics of his task faithfully and completely. We can see a logical method: the theme is that the gospel is power (Romans 1:16); the need for this is for all men (Romans 3:10); the solution is Christ (Romans 3:25). Paul teaches us that man cannot earn his salvation—all religions that attempt salvation by works cannot succeed. The only path of salvation is that of faith. Each man is restored to God individually, and that is through the manifest grace of God in Jesus Christ. The first eleven chapters deal with the issue of salvation, and from Chapter 12 through 16 Paul gives ethical applications of what it means to have this salvation.

At this point, I would like to encourage each student to stop and consider what God has done for us. God makes it very clear in His Word that we are all sinners and that we are separated from Him.[63] This separation will eventually lead to an eternal punishment in hell[64]; however, God in His infinite wisdom, mercy, and love has provided a means by which we can be restored into relationship with

Him. This means is by the death of His Son upon the cross at Calvary.[65] If we put our trust in what Christ did for us, if we believe on Him and call upon Him, the Bible says that God's grace will be ours; we will have eternal life and live eternally with Him.[66] Friend, have you settled this with God? If not, please take a moment now and pray; ask Jesus to be your Savior. Then share that with your pastor, instructor, or any other Christian friend.

B. 1, 2 Corinthians

One vital truth about Paul we need to see is that when Paul started a local Church, he kept in contact to see that they continued to walk in the right way. Even as he was teaching and building new churches, Paul would take time to write to the ones he had helped establish to root them in the firm foundations of the faith.

During his stay at Ephesus, Paul wrote to many of them. It was here that he wrote to the Church at Corinth. The Church at Corinth was a vexing problem to Paul because of its instability. It was composed mainly of Gentiles without any background in the Scriptures. They had come out of some of the vilest and basest forms of religious worship of that day.

Paul, Apollos, and Peter had all at one time or another preached and worked with this group. Divisions had cropped up within the group, with factions claiming the different leaders as their champions. This, with the misunderstandings from the base, vile background, caused many struggles within that local Church.

While on the missionary tour that took him back to Palestine and then to Ephesus, Paul apparently wrote a letter to the Church at Corinth. He makes an allusion to this in 1 Corinthians 5:9. The moral atmosphere of Corinth was such that an absolute separation from evil was necessary—if the Church was to survive. The full content of the previous letter will never be known, for God in His wisdom did not preserve it for us.

The response to this first letter was quite unsatisfactory. Apollos and Peter had moved on to other fields, and the Church was left with little leadership. Three of the members, Stephanos, Fortunatos, and Achaicus, brought a contribution to Paul and a letter containing questions, which the Corinthians wanted clarified. In response to these circumstances, Paul wrote what we call 1 Corinthians. The letter was probably written in the winter of 55 AD during the prosperous peak of his work at Ephesus.

1 Corinthians is the most varied in content of all of Paul's writings. The topics range from schism to finance, from Church decorum to the resurrection. Paul uses many literary devices in this letter. There is logic, sarcasm, entreaty, scolding, poetry, narratives, and exposition. The style closely resembles that of Paul having a conversation with them. The main theme of this letter is Christian conduct, and the problems discussed are by no means outdated. These problems can still be found anywhere Christians come into close contact with a pagan civilization.

Chapter 7, verse 1 shows that the last half of this book is written in response to their questions. Each problem in this letter is not met by applying a psychological expedient, but by the application of a scriptural principle. He told them the remedy for schism in the Church was spiritual maturity. In areas of fornication, Church discipline was advised. For litigation among Church members, they were to take their problems to the Church not the local constable.

This letter was dispatched to Corinth by Timothy, possibly sent along to help straighten out any other problems within the Church. After a period of time, revival does break out in the Church where they change their attitudes from that of carelessness and obstinacy to one of repentance.

The letter of 2 Corinthians deals mainly with personal matters rather than with doctrinal or ecclesiastical issues. The human side of Paul is prominent. Here we see some of his feelings, his desires, dislikes, ambitions and obligations. This affords us an insight into the career of Paul that none of the other epistles gives. It appears to be written not only to defend him against the occasional criticisms of the Corinthian Church, but also the slanders and accusations that his enemies had raised against him.

The picture drawn from the inference of the writings of these two letters lets us see that the churches in the Apostolic Age had their struggles and sins also. We must also learn from the situation at Corinth that while there can be real struggles and incorrect situations within a Church, but this does not mean they are no longer a Church of Jesus Christ. This Church at Corinth had many, many flagrant violations of the teaching of the apostles, yet Paul never stops praying, teaching, and helping them. Does there come a time when God removes a Church from His role? Yes, the Bible in Revelation teaches that, but Corinthians teaches us that we do not make that decision—God does.

C. Galatians

The letter to the Galatian churches was one of two letters in the Scripture that could be called protest literature. These were written shortly before the Council of Jerusalem mentioned in Acts 15. The other letter is James, and that will be covered in Chapter 8. They deal with the protest, or controversy, of legalism versus liberty in the first century churches.

Galatians was written by a champion of freedom who saw that neither Jews nor Gentiles could be delivered from their sins by self-effort in keeping a set of ethical principles or the Law. It has been called the "Magna Carta" of spiritual emancipation[67] because it declared that "Christ hath redeemed us from the curse of the law, being made a curse for us: For it is written, cursed is every one that hangeth on a tree: that the blessing of Abraham might come on the Gentiles through Jesus Christ; that we might receive the promise of the spirit through faith."[68]

Galatia (Gaul-atia) is the name given to the territory in north central Asia Minor where the invading Gauls settled in the third century BC. Territory came under Roman rule in 25 BC. The title is of a large region comprising of the northern section and the southern section. The question of which of these two regions Paul wrote about has been debated for years. The southern Galatian theory sets the letter as being sent to the churches founded on Paul's first missionary journey. This allows for an early date of writing. The northern Galatian theory places the letter to those churches founded during Paul's second or third missionary journey, thus making the date of the writing will be much later. Good scholars are on both sides of the issue.

The importance comes down to the dating of the letter. The southern theory seems to make the most sense time wise, because if Galatians was not written until after Paul's second or third missionary journey, why is there no reference to the Council at Jerusalem? This Council dealt with the very issue about which Paul is writing.[69] This conclusion can also be strengthened by the internal evidence of Paul's biography. He spoke of his conversion and call to ministry in Galatians 1:15, 16. He refers to his stay in Damascus (1:17), his first visit to Jerusalem (1:18), his ministry in Syria and Cilicia (1:21), and his visit to Jerusalem with Barnabus (2:1–10), which can be equated with the "famine" visit of Acts 11:30.

One last point, the episode of Peter's defection[70] could be much more easily explained if it preceded the Council. If then, the south Galatian theory is adopted; it means that Paul and Barnabus on their first tour preached in the cities of south Galatia, and on their return trip organized the converts into churches. After their return to Antioch, Peter came to visit, and after a group came claiming to be from James, Peter separated himself from the Gentiles. The same controversy broke out in Galatia, so on the eve of the council Paul wrote this letter to the Galatian churches to settle the issue there. If this is the scheme of things, Paul wrote the letter from Antioch just prior to the Council of 48 or 49 AD.

Galatians was written as a protest against the corruption of the gospel of Christ. The essential truth of justification by faith rather than by the works of the law had been obscured by the Judaizers' insistence that believers in Christ must keep the Law if they expected to be accepted by God. The tone of the book is fairly warlike. It crackles with indignation, not personal but spiritual. Paul cries out, "But though we, or an angel from heaven, preach any other gospel unto you than that which we have preached unto you, let him be accursed…" as reproof of the Galatians for accepting the legalistic error.

If the early date is accepted, this letter is the earliest of Paul's existing writings. It summarizes the heart of the gospel—that is that man's chief problem is obtaining a right standing with God. Christ has given us that standing, and it is not based upon our living the Law.

Paul teaches us that in Christ we have freedom—and that freedom can best be described as the liberty to do that which is right. Freedom in Christ means we have the ability and strength to do that which is right in the sight of God.

D. Ephesians

Ephesians, Philippians, Colossians, and Philemon make up the four letters of the Pauline imprisonment. These are written during the time period when Paul was under arrest and imprisoned at Rome. This makes the time frame about 60 to 62 AD. There is no doubt that they were written during his imprisonment because they all refer to his bonds.[71] The view that they were written from Rome seems correct because of Paul's reference to Caesar's household[72] and to the Praetorial guard.[73]

Ephesians was a general letter, one that was for the Church at Ephesus, but was to be shared with the other churches in the area. Paul makes mention that Aristarchus, Epaphas, Luke, and Demas were with him when he wrote this letter. Mark had rejoined Paul at this time and was contemplating a journey into Asia—so Paul commends him to the Church at Colosse. This letter was written after many churches had come into being, and Paul had given much thought to the meaning of this organism that existed.

The theme is the Church developed to remind them of the exalted position that the local Church had in God's Plan. This is not a letter about an invisible, universal mystery but one about the physical, local body of Christ. This is being sent to those who had some maturity in the faith. The first half elaborates upon the divine plan of redemption, while the second half deals with the practical conduct of the believer in relationship to the Church.

If the book of Romans is a sample of Paul's teaching that he would give on his first visit to an area, Ephesians would be his "Bible Conference." There is little theology or doctrine that cannot be found in his other writings, producing principles that are integrated into a picture of the Church as a single functioning body equipped with standards and engaged in a spiritual battle.

E. Philippians

Another of the Prison Epistles is the letter to the Church at Philippi. This is this author's favorite book in the New Testament.

The letter is the most personal of all the letters of Paul that we have today. There are over one hundred uses of the first person pronoun in this book. The Church had been intensely loyal to him, so he was able to speak freely to them of his tribulations and ambitions. They had taken a collection to help him in his time of need. Ephaphroditus had brought the gift to him and fell grievously ill. He did recover, and Paul attributed this to prayer. The date of the writing is uncertain, but it is reasonable to believe it was written close to the end of the two-year imprisonment at Rome. This would place it at around 61 to 62 AD. Two topics predominate the text of this letter. The first is the topic of the "gospel," which Paul mentions over nine times. The concept denotes a body of faith—established and in place even in this early time of the Church movement. Paul stresses the point in Philippians 2:8 that the good news is that Christ died for all men, and in 2:9 that men can possess this righteousness before God.

The second topic is that of "joy." This book written by a man in bonds carries no pessimistic ideas or attitudes. Paul stresses the point that as Christians, we have joy in the midst of circumstances and disasters. This book gives us a personal glimpse into the mind and life of Paul. To him, all life is summed up in Christ. Philippians 3 gives us an insight into the driving motivating force in the life of Paul. He pressed toward the goal of pleasing God in everything he did. His life was to please God. In turn, he is encouraging the Philippian Christians, as well as us today, to live a life wrapped up in Christ so that our joy would be beyond measure.

F. Colossians

The letters of Ephesians and Colossians are really twins. They belong together to complete each other. Where the letter to Ephesus dealt with the body of Christ—the Church—the letter to Colosse deals with the head of the Church—Christ. The town of Colosse was located in the hinterland region of Asia. It was on a rocky ridge that overlooked the valley of the Lycus River. It was a good-sized city, but it was decadent. Possibly it was evangelized by Timothy or Epaphras.[74] Paul's references in his letter point to the fact that he had never been there himself. The heresy, which evoked this letter, was a blasé form of intellectualism. This intellectualism was only interested in mysteries, secret knowledge, and wisdom. This, in turn, caused them to discount Christ as a false philosophy. Paul did not spend his time in idle theories. To him, the gospel had clear ethical consequences. To Paul, Jesus Christ was first in all things.

Paul works to build a case that Christ is preeminent in the very beginning of this letter. He shows Christ to be preeminent in creation (1:15–18), in redemption (1:20, 21), in the Church (1:18), and in our personal lives (1:22). There is not given a space for Christ not to be center. As the Church should be the body of Christ here on earth, Christ is that Head which directs all that we do through His Word and His Holy Spirit. If we as Christians truly put Christ first, what a difference that would make in our homes, churches, communities, country, and the world.

G. 1, 2 Thessalonians

These two letters chronologically belong to Paul's stay in Corinth around 52 AD. They were written within a few months of each other while Paul was engaged in his ministry in Achaia.

Thessalonica was founded about 315 BC by Cassander, who named it in honor of his wife, the half-sister of Alexander the Great. There was a Jewish colony in Thessalonica with a synagogue, and it was here that Paul preached for three weeks. He taught them from the Scriptures that the Messiah would die and rise again, and this created such a stir that Paul was forced to leave the city under the cover of night. Even with the great persecution, the Church in this city grew and became established.

1 Thessalonians had a twofold reason for being written. First, Paul wanted to praise those who were standing strong, even in the face of severe persecution by the Jews. He also wrote to correct certain errors and misunderstandings that had grown over the period of time. The main doctrinal theme is the return of Christ. It is here in this letter that we have the earliest and most complete discussion of this topic.

The people here had received Christ, learned the doctrine presented, and sought to follow Jesus. However, with the passing of time, some of their members had died. They were concerned about what happened to those who died before the Lord's coming. Had they lost out? Paul deals carefully and triumphantly with this topic. He gives great assurance that all will be taken at the Trump of God—those in the grave and those of us who remain. Paul in this passage gives us a glimpse that he was expecting Christ to return within his lifetime. He uses the phrase, "We which are alive and remain…" including himself in the living being Raptured.

After dealing with that mistaken concept, Paul is shortly forced to write to them again. This time in 2 Thessalonians, Paul writes to correct the mistaken idea that Christ had already come. Paul undertook to provide them with specific criteria to look for in the approach of the "Day of the Lord."

Apparently, according to Paul, three main events will happen at the coming of Jesus. First, there will be a sudden acceleration of apostasy from godliness (2:3). This will be taking place within the Church. The world has never been godly in and of itself. Next, there will be the removing of the restraining influence in the world (2:6, 7). This is the removal of the saved. We are like salt—preserving the world from total putrefaction. Finally, at the coming of the Lord, the incarnation of evil will be unveiled and animated by Satan (2:4, 9). This Man of Sin will oppose and exalt himself over all that is called God. The triumph will be the personal, bodily return of Christ to earth to destroy the Antichrist.

Paul also urged them to earn their own livings and to mind their own business. Many feeling that the approach of Christ was near had ceased to work. They expected everyone else to take care of them.[75] Idleness is never God's plan for His people. One of the side effects of idleness is that those with time on their hands usually become gossipers, busybodies, just plain nosy in other people's affairs. This also is not the plan of God for His people.

Paul emphasizes the truth that has been well established, even in the early period of the Church movement. This truth has stood the test of time—for it holds true today, just as it did when Paul wrote it.

H. Philemon

The last letter we will look at in this chapter is the personal letter that Paul wrote to Philemon. Philemon was a friend of Paul's, a businessman of Colosse, one who Paul knew had a relationship with the Lord. He wrote this letter at the same time that he wrote Ephesians and Colossians.

Onesimus was a slave of Philemon and had absconded with some of his master's property. He ran to Rome (where many slaves tried to hide) hoping to lose himself in the crowds. In some way Paul crossed paths with this slave and led him to Christ. Realizing the necessity of making right the wrong, Paul sent him back to his owner. With Onesimus, he sent a personal note requesting that Philemon forgive and receive Onesimus back. Paul personally offered to pay any financial loss that Philemon might have suffered.

This letter is the greatest record and teaching about forgiveness in the Bible. In this letter are found all the elements dealing with forgiveness—God with us, and ourselves with others. When dealing with forgiveness, first it is understood that there is an offense (11, 18). This is something done directly to another person. The Bible speaks clearly that we are opposed to God and that our sins have been an offense to Him. For forgiveness to come about, there must be compassion on the part of the one offended (10). It is because of the Lord's mercy that we are not destroyed. Usually there must be some form of intercession (10, 18, 19) on behalf of the individual that offended. Paul did it for Onesimus, and Christ does it for us.

Every time someone is forgiven, a price is paid. The one forgiving pays that price. Paul offered to be a substitute for the offense of Onesimus (18, 19), just as Christ became our substitute upon the cross of Calvary. The beauty of forgiveness can be seen in the restoration to favor the forgiven receives from the forgiver (15). When we are forgiven by God, we are restored to full favor and communion with God. In our spiritual forgiveness, the greatest part is that we are elevated to a new relationship with God. We are no longer servants, but sons. Paul encouraged this arrangement with Philemon (16).

Without this little letter in the New Testament, we

might never picture fully the glorious benefits we receive from the forgiveness of God.

In spite of his imprisonment, Paul's ministry was not at an end. God had transported him at the expense of the State to Rome. God housed and provided for him at the State's expense for the two years he was there. Through friends and helpers, Paul was able to keep in touch with all the churches that he had a hand in establishing. In this time of forced retirement, Paul was able to pray and contemplate the leading of God. The four prison epistles give us some of Paul's finest encouraging words. When we do not see the plan going the way we want, let us look for God's hand in it and use it for His Glory.

Following the close of the book of Acts, there is no single history available. A definable change took place in Paul after his imprisonment. He began to rely more on his younger associates to do the work. It is at this stage of his career that the Pastoral Epistles, as they are called, belong. Over the years, the genuineness of these letters has been questioned, but they bear his name, and their connection with his known biography warrants their acceptance as genuine. The vocabulary and style of these letters point to the fact that they were written by the same man in the same general circumstances.

Since the movements of Paul in these letters do not align with any of his tours in Acts, it is the inevitable deduction that they belong to a period after Acts. Paul is once again traveling freely, so we see that he is freed from the imprisonment at Rome. These letters cover a broad range of time. In 1 Timothy and Titus we observe Paul as traveling. Nevertheless, 2 Timothy pictures him as once again in prison—and nearing his execution.

Assuming that Paul was acquitted around 62 AD, we find Paul resuming his missionary activities. The organization of the churches had increased in complexity. Offices had become fixed within the local churches, and there were some who were seeking these offices for the eminence and prestige that went with them. We find in these letters the offices of Bishops/Elders (Pastors) and Deacons all mentioned. The services of the local churches all had certain regular features. Wrangling and arguments developed over the points of difference between the local churches, and so heresy became a growing danger. Paul in these three letters writes to young preachers to encourage them in the work that God had called them to do. Paul gives vital instructions that even preachers of today must heed and observe.

Of Timothy and Titus, we know the most about Timothy. Timothy was born in Derbe of a Greek father and a Jewish mother. He had been reared in the Jewish faith and taught the Scriptures from his childhood. Paul came into contact with him and made him an understudy during his second missionary journey.[76] Timothy stayed with Paul and helped in the evangelization of Macedonia and Achaia. It was probably while he helped Paul with the Church at Ephesus that Timothy became thoroughly acquainted with the work and needs of the local Church. He was with Paul during Paul's first imprisonment in Rome and after his release continued to travel with Paul until he was left at Ephesus to help straighten out the problems at that local Church. At the end of Paul's life, Timothy once again joined Paul at his imprisonment, and he himself suffered imprisonment[77] from which he was later released. Timothy is a trustworthy but not forceful character. He was at least thirty years of age when Paul assigned him to the pastorate at Ephesus.[78] We also see from Paul's letters to him that he was timid and subject to stomach ailments.

Titus we know little about. We know from this letter that Titus was led to the Lord by Paul. In addition, we can deduce a few things. Titus was left as the pastor of the local Church on the isle of Crete. He is Gentile[79] and appears to have been the stronger of the two—both spiritually and physically. Paul expresses less concern for Titus' welfare than he did for Timothy's. He was possibly the more mature and virile in personality than Timothy. Both of these men are examples for those who want to serve the Lord today in the offices of pastor, and the letters give us the instruction needed for deacons.

A. 1, 2 Timothy

The letters to Timothy are intensely personal. Written in a conversational style, they are like a father writing to a son, and in Paul's mind that is exactly what he is doing. Timothy was special to this man of God. Paul opens his letter with a reminder of the charge he had left with Timothy and about the growing problem of false doctrines, which were beginning to proliferate in the churches of that day.

Paul then proceeds to recall to Timothy his own personal call, which serves as a pattern of understanding the call into the ministry. He reminds Timothy of the great responsibility of this calling, as if he is encouraging Timothy not to quit the difficult task of being a pastor.[80] Paul in this letter teaches about public worship, Church discipline, and pastoral motivations in serving God. The final appeal he makes to Timothy in 1 Timothy as a man of God is a classic presenting the four imperatives, "flee, follow, fight, and keep,"[81] portraying the elements of ministerial life in full form.

We must adventure a guess at what happens to Paul prior to his writing the second letter to Timothy. Whether he fulfilled his desire to visit Spain is unknown and whether the early churches in North Africa and Britain are converts of his is pure conjecture leading us to observe his travels to be thus:

He stopped at Corinth where Erastus chose to remain.[82]

From there he went to Miletus where he left Trophimus ill.

From Miletus he went to Troas.

And, it appears that it was in Troas where he was arrested the second time and taken to Rome.[83]

Paul may have been arrested suddenly and taken to Rome because he mentions that he left his books behind in Troas, and that his plans had been left unfinished. The place of his arrest and the cause of his arrest are uncertain.

This letter to Timothy was Paul's last message to his helpers and friends before he was martyred. The content is an intermingling of personal sentiment and administrative policy. The general tone reveals that the local Church was fighting for its life against the malicious jealousy of Judaism and the corrupt indifference of paganism. He reminds Timothy of the power of the gospel to help each persevere in their present testings and provide the strength for future trials. God is giving through Paul an encouragement to pastors of all times to "hang tough" in the ministry. Never has the task of being a minister of God been easy, and Paul's picture in Chapter 3 of the way the world would be shows that it will get harder. However, even in the hardness of the last days there will be glowing opportunities.

The final charge that Paul gives to Timothy in Chapter 4, verses 1 through 6 is a classic and should be studied carefully by every candidate who feels called to be a minister of the Living God. It is a prime summary of the task of the man of God to proclaim the gospel in spite of opposing circumstances.

B. Titus

In chronological order, the letter to Titus follows that of 1 Timothy. Paul had left Titus to finish the establishment of the local Church on the isle of Crete and to correct some of the errors that they had. The situation in Crete was discouraging. The Church was disorganized, and the members were careless in their behavior. Perhaps Paul's preaching of grace had given them the impression that salvation by faith was unrelated to an industrious and ethical lifestyle.

In six different statements, Paul enjoins good works upon these Cretian Christians.[84] Possibly this disturbance in the Church was created by the natural tendency to ethical laxness in the Cretians themselves and from the fables and commandments handed down from Judaizers in their midst. Paul refers to them in this first chapter. He calls them godless,[85] unruly,[86] divisive,[87] and mercenary.[88]

This letter could be considered a manual of conduct for members in the Church. Paul stresses systematic theological form in the Church. There is a need to protect sound doctrine, as well as practice sound doctrine in the Church. The word *sound* implies that a recognized standard of doctrine had been acknowledged in the local churches of this time to which correct life and teaching must conform. The letter to Titus is a good summary of the doctrinal teaching of the Church as it emerged into the institutional stage of existence.

To summarize this section on the letters to these young

pastors, let us take note of four important points. First, we must be aware that the growth of heresy was very apparent in these first century churches. We often feel that it is in only our day and time that we have to deal with the false teachings of the pagan and cultic worlds. In this first century Paul (and the other writers, as we shall see in following chapters) all had to encourage the truth. Second, these letters place great stress on systematic or formulated theology. "Sound" means healthy and is usually connected with good works as well as correct principles. We must see that creed and life are never divorced from each other in the Bible. To live a life pleasing to God, it is imperative that one knows and understands the doctrines of the Bible. Anyone seeking to serve God must take time to study and acquire the truths that the Bible puts forth. God does not cherish ignorance on the part of servants.

Thirdly, spiritual vitality and conduct were more important than ritual or politics in the early Church. The missionary motive was sharply in focus. It was not as important that all churches practiced the same rituals as that they all adhered to the same creed. Lastly, we must see that in spite of the persecution and heresies of that day, the local Church continued to grow and expand.

Paul wrote to encourage his sons in the ministry—do not quit in the face of severe opposition. God uses these letters to encourage pastors and those who serve Jesus to heed the same advice. Let us keep on keeping on in the work to which He has called.

There are eight letters in the New Testament that are not written by the Apostle Paul. For seven of these letters we have the author's name, but one seems almost shrouded in mystery. Each of these letters holds importance in our walk with Jesus. From Hebrews, which shows us a picture of the Holy of Holies in Heaven, to Jude, which is the doorstep into Revelation, God instructs us in vital matters of the Christian faith.

A. Hebrews

The rapid growth of the Gentile Church was independent from Judaism both by heritage and by conviction. This could only lead to a sharp division between the two groups. The members of the Jewish Church still held to the observances of the law, although they trusted completely in the Messiah. Since all used the Old Testament as the basis of faith and practice, the issue arose over the interpretations of these Scriptures. Loyalty or defection from Judaism held a powerful influence over the outcome of missionary incentive. The letter to the Hebrews was written to deal with this dilemma. Exactly to whom this letter was sent is unknown. The recipients were strong believers; they had suffered persecution and were not novices in the faith. Some believe this letter was sent to believers in Jerusalem; others believe it went to Rome.

The author of this letter is also a great puzzle. The writer does not give his name. There are no circumstances referred to in this letter to hint at the author. We can ascertain certain facts; Hebrews 2:3 tells us that he was not an immediate disciple of Christ. We can see that he is well versed in the Old Testament because he quotes freely from the Septuagint. Chapter 13:23 points to the fact that the author was a friend of Timothy and belonged to the Pauline circle. Several names have been suggested through various scholars. Barnabus, Tertullian, and Apollos are a few. The great majority of scholars assign the authorship to Paul, but there are questions about the style and diction used. Some see Luke as the possible author, saying that he was recording possibly a sermon(s) that Paul had preached. There is no final proof on the author, but as we read and study, the inspiration and inclusion in the canon cannot be disputed.

Since the author and destination are hard to ascertain, it follows in case that the dating of this letter would also be disputed. Let us take the facts of the letter and deduce the possible dating.

The letter must have been written during the lifetime of second generation Christians,[89] with a considerable interval of time between their conversion and reception of this letter.[90] The time period must have been substantial, because the author refers to their forgetting their former ways[91] and that many of their leaders had died.[92] Chapter 13, verse 23 makes mention that Timothy had been imprisoned but was now freed. The illusions to the priesthood suggest that the Temple is still standing at this time. The tone points to the fact that persecution was very immanent. The suggested dating is between 65 and 70 AD.

The theme of this letter is built around the word *better*. It is a series of comparisons showing that God's revelation in Christ is superior to all the previous revelations. The substance had made the shadow obsolete. The arguments in this letter were to encourage people tempted to abandon their faith. They were facing the approaching pressure of persecution, and with this persecution, the possible systematic abandonment of their faith.

The letter has a series of progressive warnings—each dealing with a more radical step away from the faith. There are six perils referred to in this context. These perils are of: neglect (2:1–4), unbelief (3:7–19), disobedience (4:11–13), immaturity (5:11–6:12), rejection (10:19–31), and refusal (12:25–29). Parallel to these warnings are a series of exhortations that add a positive quality to the message.[93]

One of the major aspects of this letter is the invaluable teaching that it gives on Christ and His present ministry. In the Old Testament, there were three anointed offices—prophet, priest, and king. Jesus as the Christ (or Anointed One) must fulfill all three offices. While on earth, He was the Prophet—God's voice to man. He gave us the Word of the Lord as only He could. One day He will return as the King of kings, to rule and reign from David's throne forever. Now, He is fulfilling the office of the High Priest—the representative of man to God. This is what the author of this letter is relating to his readers. This is an excellent example of early Church teaching. It is an admirable guide for the interpretation of the types and symbols presented in the Old Testament.

Doctrinally, the letter fits with the Pauline epistles of Romans and Galatians. These three give us a great deal of detail dealing with the atonement. Salvation by faith in the sacrifice of Christ is the cry of these three letters. One interesting point with these letters is that all three refer to a passage in Habakkuk. Habakkuk 2:4 states: "...but the just shall live by his faith." Each of the letters quotes this passage and then uses it almost as a theme. Romans explains the meaning of *just*, Galatians explains *how to live*, and Hebrews explains *faith*, a trilogy explaining the heart and essence of the Christian life by faith.

B. James

In chapter six, we studied the letter to the Galatians. We ascribed this as protest literature, dealing with the controversy of circumcision and legalism. This letter must be read in parallel with Galatians to acquire the fullness of the teaching of God.

The letter is ascribed to James, the half brother of Jesus. He would have been brought up in the same home environment as Jesus and possibly was in touch with Him throughout His earthly ministry. James was not a believer during the life of Jesus[94] but was a witness of the resurrection[95] and was among those waiting for the Spirit on the day of Pentecost.[96] Upon the withdrawal of Peter from Palestine mentioned in Acts 12, James became the leader of the Jerusalem Church. He was noted for his strict observance to the law[97] and later was champion of the Jews, who felt uneasy about Paul's reputation.[98] He was the moderator of the Jerusalem council covered in Acts 15. It has been said that James spent so much time in prayer his knees became calloused—so that some referred to him as having camel's knees.

The Jewish interest of this letter is shown in the opening salutation as he greets the twelve tribes of the dispersion. The synagogue is mentioned as the place of worship, and all the illustrations are taken directly from the Old Testament. It appears from the internal evidences that the letter was written while the Church was still within the circle of Judaism. While one may not be able to prove conclusively that the letter from James was written around 45 to 50 AD, its contents fit that era very well.

James may have feared that the release from the system of the law might cause Christians to be lax and careless in their behavior. He knew that this would dishonor the name of Christ. Therefore, we find a strong emphasis upon the ethics of living the Christian life. He may have feared that the doctrine of salvation by faith may have easily degenerated into the acceptance of a creed without a corresponding holiness of life. Thus, his insistence that faith must produce results in the life of the believer.

James is like the book of Proverbs in the Old Testament, because it deals with practical applications of truth in everyday situations. In very vivid, homey language, he sets forth the ethical requirements of the Christian life.

C. 1, 2 Peter

Acts gives very few relations between the Roman government and Christianity. Political relations could hardly have been unimportant. There are several ways to explain the silence. First, as has been mentioned, Christianity is spiritual, not political in nature. In addition, Christianity grew up inside of Judaism, which was permitted and protected by the Roman government. Again, the Christians who encountered the Roman government left a favorable impression on them. Toward the end of the sixth decade, the situation began to change. The Christians had separated from Judaism, and the churches were apprehensive of what this might mean. Paul's death at this time marked a turn in policy from casual tolerance to hostile criticism.

1 Peter was written in reply to this situation. The ominous shadow of persecution was the occasion for this letter. Suffering is one of the keynotes of the letter—mentioned sixteen times. Peter urges them not to be ashamed if they suffer because of their Christianity. The letter was both a warning and an encouragement to these believers. In addition to the theme of suffering, there is the counter theme of "...the true grace of God..." (5:12). Suffering should be met with grace and should develop grace in the individual.

The author of these letters was the best known of the apostles. He was a Galilean by birth and a fisherman by trade. He came to Christ early in His ministry. A natural leader and spokesman, Jesus placed him in the inner circle of disciples and gave him special attention on several occasions. Tradition says that he was crucified head downward in Rome not later than 68 AD.

The personal experience of Peter with Christ is reflected in the letter to his friends who were in peril of impending persecution. He knew the feeling of helplessness he experienced when he realized Jesus was dead, but also the feeling of hope when Jesus rose from the grave. Five times he speaks of the suffering of Christ,[99] as if the scene of Gethesamane and the crucifixion were fresh on his mind. Peter in this letter was speaking from his heart.

2 Peter begins a shift in emphasis in the letters in the New Testament. There were many problems for the early Church in the last four decades of the first century. Constant vigilance was necessary if the truth and the faith were to be kept pure. There was a rise in false doctrines during those last forty years. Perhaps, as we consider the

heresies of the first century, we can see the false teachings of today.

2 Peter was written shortly before Peter's death in Rome about 65 to 67 AD. The threat that he is dealing with is a false teaching that seemed to deny the redemption and Lordship of our savior. Peter puts forth that the answer to error is true knowledge. The words *know* and *knowledge* appear sixteen times. There are three main sections in this letter. Peter (1) discusses the nature of true knowledge; (2) gives a prophetic denunciation of errorists and (3) points out that the only hope for the future lies in true knowledge of God's program. A chief contribution in this letter is the statement in chapter 1 verse 20 and 21, which speak about the Holy Scriptures. He emphasizes the importance of correct hermeneutics of God's Word, while reminding us that it is the words that were guided by God's Holy Spirit.

D. 1, 2, and 3 John

Because of the vocabulary and style, we can safely say that these three letters are all from the same author. In fact, it is clear that the author of these letters is the same as the author of the fourth gospel, John. The gospel was written to lead us to faith, and the first letter was written to establish the certainty of our faith.

The exact time and place of the writing of these letters is undeterminable. The most accepted view is that they were written by John to the Asian churches in the last third of the first century. A major reason for his writing was to combat the heresy of Gnosticism.

Gnosticism was a philosophy of religion built upon the premise that the spirit is good and matter is evil.

Therefore, the two cannot co-exist. Salvation in this worldview consists of escaping the world of matter into the realm of the spirit. Knowledge (Greek gnosis) is what gives us the ability for salvation. From this main error arose two conclusions. Docetism taught that Christ only seemed human. He was God and "appeared" to be human. The other error was Cerinthianism from a man named Cerinthius. He taught a form of modalism that said that God became Christ for the time that he was on earth, and then He returned to His Godhead.

John insists that Christ was audible, visible, and tangible in 1 John 1:1 that whoever denies the Father and the Son is antichrist in 1 John 2:22. This letter is keyed to his personal experiences. He seeks to induce certainty of possessing eternal life and proposes tests by which this certainty can be attained. He wants the reader to be sure of his possession.

2 and 3 John deal with the area of Church polity and discipline. 2 John is more personal than 1 John is. It is addressed to "the elect lady and her children," and this could mean a particular person he is writing to or to a special Church. The main theme is that the group that this letter was written to was in danger by false teachers, and John is encouraging them to be vigilant lest they be carried astray with the false doctrine. Basically, the same danger of ignoring the humanity of Christ and the same necessity of abiding in the truth are pressed upon the readers.

3 John is addressed to a man named Gaius, who appears to be a pastor or leader in a local Church. This letter is concerned less with theological truth and more with administrative matters. It deals with two issues—first, it deals with the issue of entertaining missionary brothers

in Christ. We as local churches are to encourage these servants of God when they visit our churches. Then, it also deals with the unkind attitude of Diotrephes. John presents the need for a severe reprimand. We must beware that the mellowness of this letter not be confused with softness or vagueness. John draws a sharp distinction between truth and falsehood; between righteousness and unrighteousness; and between light and darkness, love and hate.

In the light of the rise of heresy in the first century, these letters of John present a solid front. They were written not to win a debate but to aid and develop the Christian in his daily walk.

E. Jude

This last letter that we will examine in our study is the one entitled Jude. There is a strong similarity between this letter and the one called 2 Peter. Both are dealing with the problem of heresy. The author of this letter is mentioned in Mark 6:3, where we find that he is the brother of James and the half brother of Jesus. As with James, Jude did not believe in Jesus until after the resurrection.

As to the date and place of the writing of this letter, we find few clear indications. Most believe that it was written around 67–68 AD, and possibly from Asia Minor.

Jude gives us a clear understanding of why he wrote this letter. In verse 3 he states that he originally was going to write to them and encourage them about their salvation. However, he goes on to say he found it imperative to write and urge them to stand firm in the teachings that were once and for all times delivered to the saints. He then gives the reason for writing this letter in verse 4:

heretical teachers had slipped into the local churches. His arguments follow closely to those of 2 Peter, but the visual images that he draws are much sharper.

He wants the believers to understand that those who teach such heresy are under the condemnation of God. Jude presents to the readers three historic examples of God's judgment. He displays to the reader the instance of the unbelievers who came out of Egypt in verse 5. Verse 6 deals with the illustration of the angels who kept not their first estate,[100] while he finishes the example with the discussion of Sodom and Gomorrah.

The writer makes his point that the false teachers are ignorant, irreverent, treacherous, empty, and egotistic in their error. Jude writes in triads of thoughts. As he gives three historic examples of judgment, he also gives three descriptions of the nature of the error being taught. He says that this heresy follows Cain's error of making a bloodless sacrifice (v. 11a), the error of Balaam, who thought that God was a minister of man's convenience rather than the Lord of man's destiny (v. 11b), and that erroneous thought of Korah, who had an arrogant self-devised faith (v. 11c). One point must be made: there appears to be no desire in Jude to seek to burn heretics at the stake, but to rescue those who are deluded and bewildered—while holding a zero-tolerance base of the false teaching.

Jude is called the doorstep into Revelation, because it does warn against the coming apostasy that will infiltrate the local churches. Even in his day, there was a recognized body of doctrine in the early Church. As such, Jude saw the need to uphold this truth at all costs. To Christians of today, I believe that Jude would write the same message—stand firm for those truths that have been delivered finally to the body of believers. Stand firm on the issues of Biblical inerrancy, Virgin Birth of Christ, the Vicarious Sacrifice of Christ, the Bodily Resurrection of Jesus, and the Visible Bodily Return of Christ. Stand true to the Bible on Baptism, the Lord's Supper, Spiritual gifts, and many other doctrinal issues so at stake today.

We have the truth of God entrusted to us; we must see to it that this truth is delivered to the following generations intact and unadulterated. The next chapter will take us from the past and present into the future. We will study the eschatological apocalyptic work of John, and this author will present one view that safely interprets the work without the hype and hysteria that often follows a study of Revelation.

We now come to the final book of the New Testament. A full interpretation of this book is not in the scope of this work. There have been many varied and wild interpretations of this book throughout time. We will be studying the background, the four major interpretive schemes, and the three positions on the Millennium. The author will suggest one method of interpreting Revelation that will take away the spectacular that so often follows this book.

The book of Revelation is called Apocalyptic Literature. This is a special form of writing that tends to be produced during times of persecution and oppression. Daniel in the Old Testament is another example of this style of writing. It is characterized by an intense despair for the present circumstances, while maintaining an equally intense hope for the future. In this style of writing, we find a strong use of symbolic language, dreams, and visions. The book will use supernatural agents as God's messengers in the process of God's purpose, which is cataclysmic judgment upon evil. A book like this is usually ascribed to a prominent Biblical character.

Apocalyptic literature is not to be confused with Apocryphal literature. Apocrypha comes from a Greek word, which means "hidden or concealed." These are works written close to the time of the Scriptures, but for one reason or another were not accepted as inspired of God by the vast majority of Christians.

We will now look into this wonderfully encouraging

book—one that is optimistic while at the same time disclosing the trouble to come.

Revelation

This book closes the canon and the New Testament. It is a unique book, in that it is the only New Testament Book devoted entirely to prophecy. While it is calling to our attention the trouble to come to the world that has rejected God and His Son, it gives to those who know Christ a hope and encouragement. The title in most Bibles is The Revelation of St. John the Divine, but in actuality, it would better be called The Revelation of Jesus Christ. In addition, because of the singular continuity of this work, it should be called the Revelation, not Revelations.

The author of this book is the Apostle John. He was exiled to the isle of Patmos late in his life. Patmos was a rugged, desolate island that had salt mines located on it. Those who were sent to Patmos were sent to work in the mines as punishment. Many of the prisoners never returned.[101] There are two different schools concerning when this book was written. The first school places it during the time of Nero's persecution. They refer to such points as that the numerical value of Nero adds up to 666. It appears that much of their arguments are weak. The majority school of thought is that it was written between 90 to 95 AD. This places it during the reign of Domitian. John had been a witness to the growing hostility between the Church and the Roman state. Now, he was writing to encourage these churches with which he was acquainted.

One point that has been raised by many of the scholars studying Revelation is that some of the Greek in the work seems very awkward, this is easy to explain when we consider that the author of this work is trying to put into finite human words the futuristic scenes that were shown to him.

Most scholars divide the work into three sections, using the outline that John gives us in chapter 1 verse 19. He is told to write that which he had seen, the things that were, and the things yet to come. Another way of dividing it up in three divisions are: Chapters 1–3 cover that which was at the present, Chapters 4–19 cover the Tribulation time period, and Chapters 20–22 show us the future kingdom age. We will use this last division for our study of the interpretations of Revelation.

As was mentioned in the opening section of this chapter, there are four major views of interpreting this work. These four schools of thought are called the *Preterist, Idealist, Historical,* and *Futurist* schools. We will give a basic summary of these schools.

First, there is the *Preterist* school. It comes from the Latin word which means "past." When they view the book, they see it divided as follows. Chapters 1–3 look at the historic churches of John's day. They hold no form of prophecy or warning for us. Chapters 4–19 are symbolic of the contemporary conditions of the author's day. They also carry no form of prophecy—just a statement of the world's conditions couched in hidden language. The final three chapters are symbols of the victory we will have in Heaven. Thus, except for the last three chapters, they view everything as already having taken place.

The *Idealist* school moves everything into the realm of the present. Chapters 1–3 view historic churches that John knew. The middle section is symbolic of the struggle of good and evil throughout all ages. The last three chapters are to show us the victory of good over evil. To their way of thinking, Judgment Day is whenever a great moral issue is decided for the right. Thus, there is nothing of a prophetic or futuristic nature in this work.

The *Historical* school once again sees the first three chapters as dealing only with the local churches of John's time, and that chapters 4–19 deal with the events of history. These are stages of world history that are being played out for the reader. They place them as Rome, the Reformation time period, the rise of Mohammedanism, etc. They have nothing to do with a judgment period upon the earth. The final three chapters deal with a final judgment, including the millennium and the eternal state of man. The Historicists mainly see the prophecy as already being completed. One problem within this school is that they do not agree upon the symbolic periods—making it very confusing as to what the historical time periods are.

The final group is the *Futurist* school of thought. In the realm of Hermeneutics, this is called the historical-grammatical approach to Revelation. Those of this school of thought see the first three chapters as both historical churches in John's day, but also these are symbolic representations of the seven stages of Church history leading up to the return of Jesus Christ. They view the center chapters as prophecy of the future tribulation, the judgment on the apostate Church, and the rise of the Antichrist. The final three chapters are future with the millennial kingdom, the judgment of all wicked, and the final eternal states of all men.

In addition, one must consider the three views of the Millennium when studying the work of John. Each of these views will color the interpretation and consideration that one gives to this book. The three views are the *Post-Millennial* view, the *Amillenial* view, and the *Pre-Millennial* view. The view of the Millennium is often attacked because the word is not found in the Bible. The word *Millennium* is the Latin word for one thousand years and is not found as such in the Bible. Nevertheless, the concept of this one thousand-year reign is clearly taught. Some have recommended that this concept be called Chilism—after the Greek word for one thousand, which appears in the book.

Those who held the *Post-Millennial* view saw the one thousand years as figurative. They said that the Gospel of Christ will usher in the reign of peace in this world. This reign will last until Christ returns. Basically, the Church establishes the kingdom and welcomes back Jesus. This view ended in general with World War II. Man saw that he was not getting better, but that world conditions were getting worse.

The second view of the Millennium was the *Amillenial* view. In the Greek, any time that you added "a" to the beginning of the word, it negated the word. Thus, to them the millennium is non-existent. They teach that the concept was added later, and there is no valid reason to look for a millennial reign of Christ. To them, we are living in the millennium now, and it will be finalized when Christ comes back.

The last view is the *Pre-Millennial* view. This view states that Christ will come back at the end of the Tribulation and will set up His world kingdom, of which those of us who belong to Him will rule and reign with Him. Those who hold this view tend to be Futurists in their eschatology.

There is also the ongoing debate over the return of Christ. Will He come back before, during, or after the Tribulation? In this author's view, there are two appearances of Jesus. The first appearance will be at the Rapture, when He takes his own out of the world prior to the Tribulation. The second appearance is the true Revelation, when all will see Him as He returns with His saints to set up the Millennial kingdom. The author will acknowledge that there are good scholars and men of God on all sides of this issue. The reader is encouraged to research this further on his own.

When we study the book of Revelation, one aspect stands out—Jesus Christ is the central theme of the book. It is about the revealing of Jesus—to His saints and to the world. We must keep Him central in all that we study in this book.

The author believes that this book can best be interpreted by remembering that it is dealing with the nation of Israel again. We see God restarting the clock of Israel's history, including the fulfillment of His promises to them. If we use the Old Testament (and a Jewish mentality) when dealing with the symbols and seemingly obscure parts, we will steer away from the sensational and spiritualized interpretations.

Throughout the book, John makes use of numbers. He presents a series of items based upon the number seven. These are the seven churches, Spirits of God, seals, trumpets, thunders, bowls, major persons, and there are seven Beatitudes in the book. He also used the numbers 4, 12, 24, and 144,000. We find the 24 elders, 4 living creatures, 4 horsemen, 144,000 Jewish evangelists, 12 gates to the city, 12 foundations, and 12 kinds of fruit on the tree of life. The reader is encouraged to study the meaning of numbers in the Scriptures.[102]

To modern man, the possibilities of the Apocalypse are more realistic than at any time in the past. With the advent of computers, television, and satellites, many of the mysteries seem very plausible.

With the final promise "I come quickly," the New Testament comes to an end. The cycle is complete—from creation lost to creation regained God has played out in His word the extent of who He is, who we are, where we came from, where we are going, and the issues of sin, salvation, and the Savior. The Old Testament ended with a curse, while the New Testament ends with a glorious promise. What happened in between? The advent, birth, life, death, and resurrection of Jesus all take place between the curse and the promise. The New Testament shows us how as sin separated creations of God we can be brought back into an intimate relationship with Him through Jesus. It shows us how to get right with God and how to stay right with God. It is all through His precious Son Jesus. If the reader has not settled his or her relationship with Christ, it is this author's prayer and desire that you will.

May you be encouraged to study further into the gems that are to be mined from the depths of the New Testament.

1. Willmington, Harold. *That Manuscript from Outer Space*. 1974. Private Publishing. Lynchburg, VA. pp. 11 -14.
2. It is not the scope of this work to cover all the technical details of these discussions. The student is encouraged to pursue further study on their own.
3. 1 Corinthians 2:14
4. 2 Corinthians 4:3,4
5. 2 Peter 1:9
6. Psalm 119:130
7. 1 Peter 2:2
8. See Josh McDowell's *Evidence that Demands a Verdict* for a more complete discussion of this.
9. Luke 2:11
10. Acts 18:2
11. Matthew 24:2
12. Lord and God
13. Daniel 7: 1–7
14. Galatians 4:4. This is a good verse to memorize. It is an excellent summary of this section.
15. John 8:33
16. Matthew 2:1–18
17. Luke 13:32
18. See Acts 12
19. Acts 25:13–26:32
20. Acts 22:25–28

21. The account of Philemon is an excellent example.
22. 1 Corinthians 15:32
23. Acts 22:3
24. Acts 18:3
25. Referred to as the penny or shilling in the KJV.
26. John 6:7
27. Acts 27:6
28. Luke 11:19
29. Acts 19:19
30. Many scholars now believe that the Ark still is in existence, hidden below the city of Jerusalem.
31. Matthew 27: 51
32. Much of the information on the feasts was gleaned from *Israel's Holy Days* by Daniel Fuchs. Loizeaux Brothers. Neptune, New Jersey.1985
33. Acts 22:3
34. Tenney, Merril C. *New Testament Survey*. 1961. Wm. B. Eerdmans. Grand Rapids, Michigan. Pg. 100.
35. John 21:25
36. Luke 5:27
37. Mark 2:14
38. Matthew 9:9
39. Mark 2:15
40. "Introduction to the book of Matthew." *The Open Bible Expanded Version*. KJV. Nelson Publishers. 1985
41. Acts 12:25 - 13:5
42. Acts 13:13
43. 2 Timothy 4:11
44. See Luke 4:38,39; 8:43; 22:44
45. Luke 1:1 - 4
46. Mark 3:17
47. Luke 9:54

48. Because of his emphasis about love in his writings, particularly in 1 John.

49. John 1:1, 14

50. John 20:30, 31—this is the explanation of why John wrote this book.

51. For a fuller discussion of this topic see Albert Garner's *Defense of the Faith*, pp. 107 - 123.

52. Greater detail can be found in many good books about Acts. Homer Kent's *Jerusalem to Rome* is one suggested work.

53. 1 Corinthians 3:16; 6:19

54. Acts 22:3

55. Acts 22:19,20

56. Acts 17:11

57. Also called the Aeropagus.

58. See 1 Corinthians 2:3

59. Garner, Albert. *Romans & Galatians* 1979. Daniels Publishing Co. Orlando, FL. pg. vii

60. Tenney, Merrill C. *New Testament Survey* 1961. Wm. B. Eerdmans Publishing Co. Grand Rapids, Mich. pg. 303. Paul states in Romans 15:19 that he had preached as far as Illyricum, and that he was on his way to Jerusalem.

61. Romans 1:13

62. McClain Alva J. *Romans* 1973. BMH Books. Winona Lake, Indiana, pg. 92

63. Romans 3:10,23

64. Romans 6:23

65. Romans 5:8

66. Romans 10:9,10,13

67. Garner, Albert. *Romans & Galatians*. 1979 Daniels Publishing Co. Orlando, FL. pg. 343

68. Galatians 3:13, 14
69. Ashcraft, Robert. *Study Guide for Galatians*. 1989. D&M Composition. Benton, Ark. pg. v
70. Galatians 2:11 ff
71. Philippians 1:12,13; Ephesians 3:1; 4:1; 6:20; Colossians 1:24; Philemon 1
72. Philippians 4:22
73. Philippians 1:13
74. Willmington, Harold. *Willmington's Guide to the Bible*. 1983. Tyndale House Publishers. Wheaton, Ill. pg. 474
75. 2 Thessalonians 3:6 - 11
76. Acts 16:1 - 3
77. Hebrews 13:23
78. 1 Timothy 4:12
79. Galatians 2:1 - 3
80. 1 Timothy 1:18; 4:6,12,16; 5:21; 6:11,20
81. 1 Timothy 6:11,12,14
82. 2 Timothy 4:20
83. 2 Timothy 4:13
84. Titus 1:16; 2:7,14; 3:1,8,14
85. Titus 1:16
86. Titus 1:10
87. Titus 1:11
88. Titus 1:11
89. Hebrews 2:1–4
90. Hebrews 5:12
91. Hebrews 10:32
92. Hebrews 13:7
93. Hebrews 4:1,11,14,16; 6:1; 10:22,23,24; 12:1,28; 13:13,15
94. John 7:2–8
95. 1 Corinthians 15:7

96. Acts 1:14
97. Galatians 2:12
98. Acts 21:17–26
99. 1 Peter 2:23; 3:18; 4:1,13; 5:1
100. It is not in the scope of this work to detail the views of the meaning of this particular issue. The reader is advised to search out this topic if further information is wanted.
101. Walvoord, John F. *The Revelation of Jesus Christ.* 1966. Moody Press. Chicago. pg. 41.
102. The student is encouraged to seek out books such as Bullinger's *Numbers in Scripture* for further study.

Archer, Gleason L., Jr. A Survey of Old Testament Introduction. Chicago: Moody Press, 1974.

Ashcraft, Robert. Study Guide for Matthew. Benton: Benton Printing, 1991.

Ashcraft, Robert. The Pastoral Epistles. Little Rock: D&M Composition, 1987.

Ashcraft, Robert. Study Guide for Galatians. Benton: D&M Composition, 1989.

Ashcraft, Robert. Study Guide for Hebrews. Benton: Benton Printing, 1992.

Ashcraft, Robert. Study Guide for Ephesians. Benton: D&M Composition, 1990.

Ashcraft, Robert. Study Guide for Romans. Benton: Benton Printing, 1992.

Bullinger, E. W. Figures of Speech Used in the Bible. Grand Rapids: Baker Book House, 1968.

Cairns, Earle E. Christianity Through the Centuries. Grand Rapids: Zondervan, 1981.

Carson, D. A. The King James Version Debate. Grand Rapids: Baker Book House, 1979.

Davis, Harold. Christian Doctrine. Henderson: TBI Class Book, 1976.

Fuchs, Daniel. Israel's Holy Days. Neptune: Loizeaux Brothers, 1985.

Garner, Albert. Bible Analysis. Texarkana: Bogard Press, 1956.

Garner, Albert. Garner-Howes Commentaries. 16 volumes. Lakeland: Blessed Hope Foundation, 1980 - 1984.

Garner, Albert. Defense of the Faith. Texarkana: Bogard Press, 1962.

Geisler, Norman. A Popular Survey of The Old Testament. Grand Rapids: Baker Book House, 1977.

Gillentine, E. C. Baptist Doctrine. Texarkana: Bogard Press, 1949.

Glover, C. N. Exposition of Revelation. Texarkana: Bogard Press, 1976.

Gower, Ralph. The New Manners and Customs of Bible Times. Chicago: Moody Press, 1987.

Griffith, J. W. A Manual of Church History. 2 volumes. Texarkana: Bogard Press, 1974 - 1976.

Ironsides, H. A. Romans. Neptune: Loizeaux Brothers, 1928.

Ironside, H.A. Lectures on the Revelation. New York: Loizeaux Brothers, 1919.

Jensen, Irving L. Jensen's Survey of the Old Testament. Chicago: Moody Press, 1978.

Jensen, Irving L. Jensen's Survey of the New Testament. Chicago: Moody Press, 1981.

Keller, Werner. The Bible As History. New York: Morrow, 1956.

Kent, Homer A., Jr. Jerusalem to Rome. Grand Rapids: Baker Book House, 1972.

LaHaye, Tim. Revelation. Grand Rapids: Lamplighter Books, 1975.

Lockyer, Herbert. ED. Nelson's Illustrated Bible Dictionary. Nashville: Nelson, 1986.

Lockyer, Herbert. ED. The Open Bible Expanded Version. Nashville: Nelson, 1985.

May, Herbert G. ED. Oxford Bible Atlas. New York: Oxford University Press, 1974.

Morris, Henry. The Revelation Record. Wheaton: Tyndale House, 1983.

McClain, Alva J. Romans. Winona Lake: BMH Books, 1973.

McDowell, Josh. Evidence That Demands a Verdict. San Bernadino: Here's Life Publishers, 1979.

McDowell, Josh. More Evidence That Demands a Verdict. San Bernadino: Here's Life Publishers, 1981.

McElmurry, Tom. The Key of the Bottomless Pit. Texarkana: Bogard Press, 1987.

McElmurry, Tom. The Tribulation Triad. Texarkana: Bogard Press, 1983.

Newell, Wm. R. The Book of the Revelation. Chicago: Moody Press, 1935.

Pentecost, J. Dwight. Things to Come. Grand Rapids: Zondervan, 1958.

Ramm, Bernard, Protestant Biblical Interpretaton. Grand Rapids: Baker Book House, 1970.

Robertson, A. T. A Harmony of the Gospels. New York: Harper & Row, 1950.

Scofield, C. I. The Scofield Refence Bible. New York: Oxford University Press, 1945.

Strong, James. Exhaustive Concordance of the Bible. McLean: MacDonald, N.D.

Tenney, Merril C. New Testament Survey. Grand Rapids: Eerdmans, 1961.

Tenney, Merril C. John, The Gospel of Belief. Grand Rapids: Eerdmans, 1976.

The Open Bible Expanded Version, King James Version. Nashville: Thomas Nelson, 1985.

Vine, W. E. An Expository Dictionary of New Testament Words. Old Tappan: Revell, 1966.

Virkler, Henry A. Hermeneutics. Grand Rapids: Baker Book House, 1981.

Walvoord, John F. The Revelation of Jesus Christ. Chicago: Moody Press, 1966.

Wilkinson, Bruce. Talk Thru the New Testament. Nashville: Thomas Nelson, 1983.

Willmington, Harold. Willmington's Guide to the Bible. Wheaton: Tyndale House, 1983.

Willmington, Harold. That Manuscript From Outer Space. Lynchburg: Private Publishing, 1974.

Willmington, Harold. Willmington's Survey of the Old Testament. Wheaton: Victor Books, 1987.

Willmington, Harold. The King Is Coming. Wheaton: Tyndale House, 1973.

Thomas Marshall is a minister, Christian Education administrator, educator, and family man. He has been privileged to teach the Bible to students of all ages and has presented seminars at the Association of Christian Schools International, Washington, D.C. conventions on how to teach the Bible. His motto is "It is a sin to bore people with the Bible." Dr. Marshall has degrees from Liberty University, Johns Hopkins University, Andersonville Theological Seminary, Texas Baptist Institute and Seminary, as well as other institutions. He is currently working toward a Master of Divinity degree from Liberty Theological Seminary in Lynchburg, VA. He has earned Professional Lifetime Educational Certification with the ACSI in the areas of All-levels Principal, Secondary Bible Teacher, and Bible Specialist. His hobbies include reading, spending time with his family, playing guitar, walking, and being a life-long student.

He resides in Silver Spring, MD with his wife of 36 years, Linda. Dr. Marshall is currently the Lower School Principal at Montrose Christian School in Rockville, MD, where his wife is the Admissions Director for the Montrose Christian Child Development Center. Together they have three wonderful daughters and two outstanding granddaughters. Deborah, along with her husband, Kevin Poole, live in Lynchburg, VA, and have two magnificent daughters, Kaylah and Madison. Grace, is employed by the ABC Television affiliate in Washington, D.C., Comcast, and ESPN Sports. Joy, is a student at Liberty University majoring in English.